Webcam Savvy

For the Job
or
The News

By

Clarence Jones

THIRD EDITION

Webcam Savvy
For the Job or the News

by Clarence Jones

Third Edition
(also available as an e-book)
ISBN-13: 978-1542869140
ISBN-10: 1542869145

Published by:

Clarence Jones
6907 Vista Bella Dr.
Bradenton, FL 34209
Voice: 941.779.0242
e-mail: cjones@winning-newsmedia.com

Other books by Clarence Jones

Winning with the News Media -
   A Self-Defense Manual When You're the News

They're Gonna Murder You -
   War Stories from My Life at the News Front

Filming Family History -
   Saving Great Stories for Future Generations

Sailboat Projects -
   Clever Ideas and How to Make Them

More Sailboat Projects - A Sequel
   Clever Ideas and How to Make Them

Table of Contents

Prime Example of a
Terrible Webcam Interview

This is taken from a real interview aired by a TV network. In color, it's even worse than it appears here. Everything is tinged blue or pink.

7:33|56°

Nothing in the video seems to be in focus. The network logo, time, and local temperature in the lower right are sharp, but they were superimposed over the webcam image.

It appears to have been shot with a laptop webcam in a motel room.

Awful. Truly awful.

So bad, viewers probably didn't hear a word this guy spoke. The Gettysburg address would have been overwhelmed by the miserable setup.

Keep reading. I'll show you how to avoid this kind of debacle.

Preface

If you want to succeed in that next webcam job audition or news interview, it takes some preparation. And work. It's not as easy as it seems. To get the job - or to get your point across in a news story - you'll need a lot of webcam savvy.

If you don't have the gear and skills, you'll wind up at the unemployment office (if you were auditioning for a job) or on the cutting room floor (of the network or local TV station).

You need to look and sound self-confident, relaxed, sincere, and unrehearsed. That takes a lot of practice. Very few of us are born with it.

You also need to use the right webcam, background and lights. You can set it up easily for less than $200.

We have become so accustomed to slickly produced video, you scream AMATEUR-BEGINNNER if the interview was:

- Filmed with a low-quality webcam
- Shot at a strange angle
- Poorly framed
- Badly lit, with a cluttered background of
  - Debris and the sound of a
  - Crying baby or a barking dog

Once you understand the basics, you need to practice, practice, practice. That's what it takes to see and hear yourself on camera the way you want others to see and hear you.

And to change what needs to be changed.

They're Saving Money

Webcam interviews are rapidly becoming the norm for many business, news, and government agencies. They save a lot of staff time and money.

Corporations use webcams to interview prospective employees. Or for conversations with staff in distant parts of the world.

Both network and local newscasts use them to interview witnesses, or experts who explain the background of a story.

In terms of cost and convenience, webcam interviews are great. In terms of quality, they're often lousy. They're today's equivalent of kids playing telephone with tin cans connected by a string.

Better, Inexpensive Equipment

It's not always the equipment at fault. The electronic gear available today is very good, and inexpensive. But many of the people on camera don't realize that much better webcams are available, or how to use them well.

TV news wins (if saving money is their goal) but YOU CAN BE THE LOSER if you're the one being interviewed.

Amateurish, Sometimes Weird

Compared to the slick packaging of TV news, the webcam interview can look amateurish and cheap. If you don't know what you're doing, you can look absolutely weird. Like the guy at the front of this book.

But the bean counters at corporate headquarters (both inside and outside the news business) are ecstatic about the money webcam interviews save. So they will continue to multiply.

For Jobs, No Travel, No Deception

The biggest saving for job interviews? No travel costs.

The business doesn't have to fly you in for the job interview, and put you up in a hotel.

If you're the interviewee and already have a job, you don't have to design an elaborate cover to hide your job hunting from your present employer.

For TV, No Crew & Expensive Gear

TV news doesn't have to dispatch a reporter and a photographer (plus in some shops, a sound technician) lugging about $75,000 worth of camera, lighting and sound gear.

With a webcam interview, the reporter or anchor sits at a desk to do the interview. No expensive equipment is necessary. An interview that might have required days of travel for a crew can be done in a few minutes.

Early Adopters

Beginning in the fall of 2010, ABC network news was one of the first (above) to regularly use webcams for news interviews.

Now local stations and all the networks are doing it.

But there's still a major problem - the poor performance of amateurs who don't know how to use their equipment, or communicate on camera.

That's the primary reason I wrote this book. To help the folks being interviewed. More about that later.

Misleading Webcam Filter

Corporations realize the webcam process is flawed, and often use the webcam as a filter to eliminate those that obviously don't fit what they're looking for.

They still use face-to-face interviews for the finalists. But that process sets up a new dynamic.

The job they're trying to fill may have nothing to do with on-camera skill or presence. Some of the prospects may be exactly what the company is looking for. But their performance and the quality of the webcam interview are so miserable, they're immediately eliminated.

Simple Solutions

Here's an example of a simple thing (above) that enhances the quality of a webcam conversation. Notice how this network correspondent has used two books to raise her laptop on the desk so the tiny camera built into the top rim of her laptop screen will be at the correspondent's eye level.

Crude, but it works.

Phone Interviews with Bad Video

Let's face it. Many webcam interviews are just phone conversations with badly-lit, jerky, out-of-focus, off-color video.

And audio that sounds like the mike was in the next room. The words we hear are not in synch with the moving lips. Both video and audio drop out intermittently.

All of these problems can be solved easily at very little cost.

In a national survey years ago, a national association of radio and television news directors asked its members how they would define "investigative reporting."

One memorable reply:

"Grainy, out-of-focus film."

With webcam interviews, it's déjà vu all over again.

You Won't Like the Way You Look

If you've been interviewed in person by a TV news crew (reporter, photographer, broadcast-quality camera, lights and microphone) you probably didn't like the way you looked and sounded. Even with all those pros and expensive gear.

Just wait until you see and hear yourself when you're Skyped for a newscast.

TV Interviews Unfair

TV news interviews in person have always been unfair. Stress can look like guilt, or fear, or deception. The same is true for job interviews.

In a webcam interview, add to stress the distortion of a bad camera, mike, and Internet connection, accompanied by Halloween-type lighting and a junky background.

This scenario has all the ingredients for a true disaster - for your career, your point of view, and your self-esteem.

Job Interview Fairness

During the research for this book, I came across an Internet discussion where a professor had applied for a job in another state. He did not get the job. He blamed his failure on the webcam interview process.

Local applicants for the job were interviewed in person, he said. Only out-of-towners were interviewed by webcam. A local got the job. This out-of-towner was bitter about how the webcam process had stacked the deck.

Rent a Webcam

Consulting companies are popping up that will take over the process for an organization that wants better results from webcam interviews of job prospects.

For a fee, the specialty service company overnights a high-quality webcam and microphone to the interview candidate, with detailed instructions on how to set them up. After the event, the equipment is shipped back to the consultants.

Even with the consulting company's fee, the hiring company spends a lot less than they would for in-person interviews.

A New Survival Skill

Even if you have top quality equipment, you're still at a disadvantage. For great webcam presence, you need to know how to use it. And practice. Webcam savvy is rapidly becoming a survival skill.

To get up to speed and be ready for this kind of interview, you may need to spend roughly $150 to $200 on a high-quality webcam, a tripod, perhaps an external microphone, and some auxiliary lights.

And Now, the Good News

Surprisingly, the latest webcams have improved so much, they approach broadcast quality. But whatever you buy, you need to know how to set it up the way the pros would.

Even if you're intimidated by electronics and computers, you'll find the new webcams incredibly easy to use.

But just plugging a webcam into your computer and turning it on won't cut it. In the following pages, I'll show you how to create winning webcam interviews.

What's Ahead

- Why a fast computer and Internet connection are crucial
- Choosing the right webcam
- How and where to buy it at the best price
- Installing and setting it up
- How to light your set
- Creating a background to reinforce your message and not distract from it
- Ways to make viewers like, believe, and trust you
- How great webcam interviews can create better public relations and
- How you can become the "expert on call" when TV news needs a quick interview

It's free advertising. Good for business or your practice. Builds confidence from your clients or patients. IF it's done well. Let's get started.

The Technical Stuff

Good webcam interviews need these basic elements:

- A powerful computer
- High-speed internet connection
- High-quality webcam and the right framing
- High-quality microphone (which may be built-in)
- Good lighting
- Background that doesn't distract
- On-camera skills

Laptop Webcams

The webcams built into most laptops are not very good. Measuring the quality can get complicated, but here's a crude way to check:

Take a still picture with your laptop webcam. Then look at that picture in a photo editing program; Windows® File Explorer; or Finder, the program that shows files in an Apple® computer. With your cursor over the file name, right click it.

A menu list will drop down. Left click PROPERTIES. You'll see a lot of stuff about the photo, including its dimensions in pixels. Pixels are the tiny dots that make up the photograph. The more pixels, the higher the image quality.

How to Measure Quality

Multiply the vertical pixels by the horizontal pixels. Most laptop webcams will shoot about photos of about 2 MP (each photo contains two million pixels).

By comparison, my separate USB webcam shoots 10 MP photos. That's five times more resolution that the usual laptop webcam.

The digital camera I use for serious photography produces 20 MP photos.

Be aware the dimensions of a still photograph shot by a webcam may not be the same as the video it shoots. This is just a rough way to compare the quality of the webcam you're using, with the one you might decide to buy. More about that in a moment.

The Computer

Your computer needs to be fairly new, and fast enough to process and transmit the video/audio signal your webcam produces. Here's how to find out what's inside the guts of your computer case:

- If you have a Windows machine, go to CONTROL PANEL and click on SYSTEM.
- For an Apple computer, go to ABOUT THIS MAC.

Take Notes on Your System

Write down what you see there, because you'll need to know these things to make sure the webcam you shop for is compatible with your computer:

- Central Processing Unit (CPU) type and clock speed in GHz (gigahertz)
- Amount of RAM (random access memory) installed in GB (gigabytes)
- Operating System (OS) type

Windows comes in 32-bit and 64-bit versions.

Macs will show the Operating System (OS) as a name and number.

My desktop has an Intel® Quad Core™ CPU with a clock speed of 3.3 GHz. It's running Windows 10 (the 64-bit version) and has 16 GB of RAM. I built it from scratch, and it is powerful.

Don't Be Intimidated

Don't be intimidated by the geek terms. You don't need to understand what they mean. Just be sure the webcam you buy will work with your computer. If you want to use the best new webcam, you may need a better computer.

One of the hurdles for webcam interviews is what we have come to expect from watching TV news. Broadcast-quality cameras cost more than $50,000.

They produce VERY sharp video (unless the aging reporter or anchor tells the photographer to shoot slightly out of focus to blur the wrinkles). TV news cameras have near-perfect color balance, and true-to-life audio.

Webcams for Grandma & Lovers

Webcams and programs like Skype® and Face Time® were invented to let Grandma see and talk to the grandkids half-way across the country. Or so young lovers could chat and see each other while they talk.

No need for anything fancy. Just a low price. Most Grandmas and young students have limited budgets.

More Sophisticated Now

As industry began to realize webcam possibilities, more sophisticated webcams came to market. And as the quality increased, so did the price.

But mass sales have brought the prices down. My Logitech C920 (considered by most reviewers to be one of the best available) now costs about $70 online.

It has full HD capability, with 1080p resolution (1080 lines of pixels from top to bottom). I can choose HD screen proportions (9x16) or the old, standard proportions (2x3).

Search on the Internet

Begin your search for a webcam on the Internet. Using your favorite search engine, look for "best webcams." Read reviews published by technical magazines and blogs.

Once you've narrowed the list down to three or four webcams the reviewers recommend, go to websites that sell those models. Read reviews by owners who bought them there.

I'll recommend merchants in the chapter on *Buying Your Webcam*. Remember - you get what you pay for.

Don't Buy What You Don't Need

There are lots of webcam features out there you may never use. Here are the basic specifications I recommend for high-quality webcam interviews:

- <u>USB connection</u> - This is the easiest way to connect the webcam to your computer. With one cable, you just plug it in. Most webcams have a built-in microphone designed to pick up your voice and suppress background noise. USB 3 is about 40 times faster than USB 2. But to take advantage of the faster speed, your computer must have plug-in sockets for third-generation USB. USB 3 is backwardly compatible. Most webcams work fine with USB 2.

- <u>Compatibility with your computer's OS</u> -This is why you need to know the basic system information for your computer. Some webcams will not work with some Apple or Linux® operating systems. Or an older Windows operating system. Be sure to look for comments on OS compatibility in the user reviews at merchant websites.

- <u>Auto focus</u> - This keeps the camera focused sharply on whatever is at the center of the screen, no matter how far away it is from the camera. With some models, you can switch to manual focus and sharpen the picture by turning a ring on the lens or by moving a slider switch onscreen with your mouse. The least expensive webcams have a fixed-focus lens that will provide a fairly sharp picture within a certain distance bracket. There's nothing you can do to sharpen it.

- <u>Ability to record at least 720p</u> (720 horizontal lines of onscreen pixels) - True HD (high definition) video is 1080p, but in many cases something in your data pipeline may prevent more than 720p from squeezing through. Your audio/video signal can be no faster or detailed than the slowest point in the data pipeline that transmits the webcam audio and video to the Internet.

- <u>Zoom lens</u> - This enables you to zoom in or out, and decide how much you want to capture in your webcam shot. Without it, the only way to control this is to move the webcam closer or farther away. Zooming is much better. It lets you sit farther away from the webcam but still fill the frame, so you won't be distorted, with an enlarged nose that appears to be pressed against the lens.

- Capable of taking still photos of at least 2 MP - With video editing software, you can pull a still photo from the video. With most webcams, you can take a still picture by pushing a button or clicking your mouse. Some webcams even give you a countdown on screen. In case you're taking your own picture, this gives you time to pose for the shot.

- Capable of producing at least 30 fps (frames per second) video - Some webcam video is jerky and out of synch because the webcam and computer are not capable of more than 15 fps. Movies and video are simply a series of still photos that flash very quickly and give us the illusion of movement. Thirty fps will give you smooth Internet video.

- A tripod socket - The webcam needs a tripod mounting socket. Many use a clamp that clips to the top of the monitor. You'll also need a small tripod that can sit on your desk in front of your monitor.

The Microphone

Many webcam interviews sound like the subject was in the shower and the microphone was out in the hallway. The closer to your mouth, the higher the quality of the sound it produces.

Some built-in webcam mikes are specially designed to grab sound that's 16 to 20 inches away (about the distance from your monitor to your mouth) and muffle background noise. Some even have two microphones to deliver more natural, stereo sound.

You can buy a top-of-the line webcam with a very good integrated microphone for less than it costs to buy a medium-priced webcam and a separate microphone. It's also easier to install a webcam, if the software and USB connection automatically merge audio and video.

Even so, for the highest quality audio, a microphone closer to your mouth will do a better job. A small, clip-on mike, available online for about $30, is ideal.

Origin of the Sound

It will plug into the audio input jack of your computer. You'll have to set your sound system software so it knows where the audio is coming from.

They also make headsets like the ones sportscasters use, with a mike that comes around from one side and is positioned very close to your mouth. TV anchors and sportscasters often wear this kind of mike to minimize background noise. A clip-on is easier to use.

Try a webcam with a built-in microphone first. If you don't like what you hear, experiment and spend the money for a better solution.

The Internet Connection

The speed of your Internet connection is critical for great camcorder interviews. To be successful, you MUST have a fast connection.

Since the Internet was created, computer users have focused on download (receiving) speed. In the early years, ordinary computer users rarely uploaded (sent) data.

There was no Internet, e-mail or digital photography in the Dark Ages of computers. Nearly everyone now uploads photos and large documents to websites, or attached to e-mails. That makes upload speeds much more important.

Uploads 10 Times Slower

But most Internet service providers (ISPs) designed their systems around download speeds, not uploads. Their upload speeds are usually about one-tenth the download speeds. When you transmit video and audio with your webcam, you're uploading the data to the Internet.

Telephone Dial-Up Won't Work

At the beginning of the computer age telephone lines let computers connect to one another. There are a few people in very isolated areas of the United States who still connect by telephone, but telephone modems can download data no faster than 56 kb/s (56,000 bits per second). More often, at less than 35 kb/s (35,000 bits per second).

That means upload speed of about 3.5 kb/s (3,500 bits per second). Not nearly fast enough for webcam interviews. Even those who use a satellite system to connect from isolated areas may find their speed marginal for good webcam audio and video.

Don't worry about exactly what all this means. Everything that measures speed in the computer world is relative – compared to what?

Minimum Upload Speed

The best webcams today recommend an upload speed of at least 1 Mb/s (1 million bits per second). Even the slowest cable connections offer upload speeds several times faster. The cable company I use provides 1.5 Mb/s uploads for its slowest, cheapest Internet connection service.

I pay extra to get 100 Mb/s downloads and 10 Mb/s uploads.

However you connect to the Internet, you need to know your upload speed. Lots of websites can measure that for you, and it's free.

Use your search engine to look for "measure internet connection speed." Then go to some of the websites and follow directions.

Measuring Your Speed

The website I use most often to measure my upload and download speeds is www.speedtest.net. You should test your speed several times because speed of the same connection can vary widely.

Your Internet provider probably offers a website you can use to make sure they're providing the speed you're paying for. The higher the speed, the more they charge. And the better your webcam signal will be.

Test at Several Websites

You might also want to check your speed at four or five different testing websites. The number of people surfing the Internet and the number of people using your ISP (Internet service provider) will cause speeds to vary at different times of day and different days of the week.

At most of the speed-testing websites, they're trying to sell you something that is supposed to make your computer faster. Don't be conned. You probably don't need it. But the tests are free.

Good Lighting

The best of today's webcams can shoot in very dim light. But the better the lighting, the better the video will be. Bright lighting leads to much, crisper video and a sense of three dimensions.

In the *Lighting and Background* chapter I'll show you how the placement of your lights can vastly improve the quality of your webcam video.

Buying Your Webcam

I buy almost everything electronic online.

Online, you have the largest possible selection to choose from. Prices are lower than local stores. At many web merchants, you pay no sales tax. And they frequently offer free shipping.

Search for Reviews

If you decide to get a better webcam, the first step is to read a number of webcam reviews posted by technical magazines, blogs and forums. Search for "best webcams" or "webcam reviews."

Be aware that there may be a conflict of interest in some of these reviews. The magazine or online publication may carry advertising.

Consider the Advertising

The advertising can tilt reviews in favor of those brands. Sometimes manufacturers provide free products to be reviewed, and that can prejudice what's written about them.

You'll find that some of the best webcams are recommended by several reviewers. All of the reviewers can't be bought. When you have several highly rated models in mind, go to websites that sell those webcams.

The Manufacturer's Website

You may also want to go to the webcam manufacturer's website. There, you'll find the list price, and be able to compare the features of different models they make.

A shortcut to find good prices and who sells them is to search for "price shopping services" or "price comparison services" with your favorite search engine.

How Price-Shopping Works

On the price-shopping website, you enter the brand and model number. They tell you where that item is for sale, and at what price. Some also give you customer ratings for the merchants they monitor.

Be aware, however, that price-shopping services don't cover every merchant. And the prices they post are sometimes out of date.

I've learned to also use a search engine to look for the brand and model I want to buy. Sometimes that will turn up a merchant and a low price that's not listed by the price shopping services.

Rating Online Merchants

I rate online merchants by their:

- Low prices
- Return policies
- Customer service
- System for searching within their own website
- Collection of user reviews, and the ability to sort them (best to worst)
- Speed in shipping my order
- e-mailing me when my order is shipped, with a tracking number

Reviews by Customers

Most online merchants now collect reviews from ordinary people who have bought from them. I've come to depend on user reviews for critical information. Unless the merchant has posted phony customer reviews, they're fairly reliable.

I tend to respect reviews that include some really nasty comments while a high percentage of the reviewers praise the product. I wonder about reviews with no unsatisfied customers. I wonder if the bad reviews have been censored.

Ordinary users tell you about software conflicts and lousy technical support if they had problems with installation. Professional reviewers are often too kind, not wanting to be cut off by a manufacturer if they're too critical.

Skill Level Tilts Reviews

Professional reviewers are also highly skilled in using computers. Something that seems easy to the pros may not be so simple for those who have less computer knowledge and experience. The best of the user review systems also tell you how much technical expertise the reviewer claims.

Some of the terrible reviews often come from newbies (beginners) who simply didn't know how to install or use the equipment. Take those with a grain of salt. And understand that the best brands occasionally produce a defective item.

My Favorite Shopping Sites

My favorite websites for electronic gear are amazon.com and newegg.com. They have very good prices (especially if there's a sale or rebate) and a lot of free shipping.

You can set up an alert that will send you an e-mail if their price drops.

At almost all sites now, they remember you, once you've set up an account and ordered from them. That makes future purchases very easy.

Always Use a Credit Card

I always use a credit card for online purchases. If something goes wrong between you and the merchant, most credit card companies will stop payment until you're satisfied.

If your credit card company is not willing to be your advocate, you need to cancel that card and get another.

Many people are concerned about the security of using a credit card online. I'm much more concerned about a waiter in a restaurant copying my credit card number, then using it to increase the tip, or buy something else with the card. I've had that happen.

Credit Card Security

Most credit card companies protect their card holders from fraud. They have very good security systems. In a city away from home, I bought some clothing at two different stores one morning. When I was checking out at a third store, my cell phone rang.

The call was from American Express®, checking to make sure my card had not been stolen. I was amazed that their system had flagged the purchases, found them unusual, and contacted me.

More recently, I ordered a $300 item from a company in England. In less than a minute, the credit card company called to make sure the purchase was legitimate. Amazing.

Extended Warranties

American Express and some other cards will double the manufacturer's warranty (up to an extra year) for anything you buy with them.

I've collected on the extended warranty feature at least a half-dozen times. But beware - if you buy the merchant's extended warranty, the credit card warranty extension no longer applies.

Some merchants and some credit card companies have a price-match policy. If something you buy goes on sale within a month or so, they'll refund the difference between that and what you paid.

Unpack it Carefully

When you buy your webcam, unpack it very carefully and save EVERYTHING that came with it. If it's defective, or incompatible with your computer, you won't be able to return it unless everything that came with it goes back to the merchant.

Installing Your Webcam

First, read the directions that came with your webcam. ALL OF THEM. To save money, most electronics manufacturers no longer print long directions. The extensive instructions are either online or on the CD that comes with the product.

Don't Use the Disk Until ...

But DON'T use the enclosed CD to install the webcam until you've checked the manufacturer's website. This technology is evolving so rapidly, that enclosed disk is probably out of date.

Go to the manufacturer's website. Click on SUPPORT or DOWNLOADS. Find the file that installs your webcam on your type of operating system.

It will show a version number and a date. Compare that to the version printed on the CD. If they're the same, use the disk. If the website version is newer, download the file.

Updates Avoid Problems

Software is constantly updated to fix bugs. When enough buyers call technical support about a problem with their new purchase, the company finds what it will take to solve the problem, and releases a new version.

You can save yourself a lot of time and trouble if you have the latest version. A small program that runs a piece of computer hardware like a printer or a webcam is called a "driver."

Don't Lose the Download

If you haven't downloaded a lot of files, and set up your system to do it, it's easy to lose them. You need to know where they are when the download is finished.

Some people download to their desktop. Your browser may save all your downloads and make them easy to access. I've set up my browser (Mozilla Firefox) so that all downloads go into a folder I created - C:\Downloads.

Once a software driver is in the Downloads folder, I move it to another folder - C:\Software Updates\Manufacturer's

Name. I do it that way because I sometimes need to install the same update on several computers (I have three).

Or, if a program becomes corrupted, I can re-install it without having to download it again. When the next update is issued, I put it in that folder and delete the older file.

Once you have the driver downloaded and you know where it is, shut down all programs that are running.

Reduce the Chance of a Glitch

Having all programs turned off will reduce the chance of a glitch in the installation. Open up Windows Explorer if the file is in a folder. It may be on your desktop if you're using an Apple computer.

Put your cursor on the file name and double-click it. That will start the installation of the program. Follow the on-screen directions.

Wait to Plug In Your Webcam

Don't plug in your webcam until the installation software tells you to. Most webcams are designed to sit on top of your monitor. Put it there for the install.

With the installation finished, and the webcam plugged in, launch the program (if it's not already running). You should see yourself on screen, sitting in front of your monitor.

A star is born.

Go Through the Setup Process

The first time you turn on the webcam, most installation software will take you through a setup routine to adjust the video and audio settings. You'll have to tell the computer if you're using a microphone that's not integrated in the camera. And where it's plugged in.

Only one program can use the webcam at a time. If another program has automatically started as a result of your plugging in the webcam, you'll have to close it to make the initial settings for the webcam.

Most of the manufacturers' programs give you a chance to make a test video and then play it back. If there's no sound on the playback, you probably haven't designated the right mike or the proper audio input jack.

Installing Skype

Skype® is the leading program that connects one webcam user to another for a video call. You'll need to become a Skype member and download their software to use the service. It's free. Most TV news operations use Skype.

With your Internet browser, go to http://www.skype.com. On their website, you may have to do a little searching to find the button that downloads the program.

Video Calls are Free

Video calls between Skype members are free, no matter where they are, anywhere in the world. The Skype website is cluttered with offers for you to subscribe to their paid calling service.

Don't be confused by those ads.

Don't Pay for Regular Phone Calls

The calling service they're trying to sell you uses Skype to make a regular telephone call. The call they charge for is just a regular telephone call, to a regular telephone number, which uses your computer's speakers and microphone. At your end, it's like being on a speaker phone.

Skype calls the phone number and if someone answers, plugs the connection into your account at Skype. You pay by the minute. It's probably cheaper than using your telephone for an international call, but not free.

A Skype video call is free, and better, in my opinion.

Searching for Skype Members

Once you've signed up, you can log in and search for other Skype members by name and location, or by e-mail address. When you find a person you might want to call, put them in your Skype contact list.

With the list showing and your webcam plugged in, clicking on the contact's name turns on your webcam and makes the call.

Placing or Answering a Call

If they're at their computer, with Skype running in the background, you'll connect almost instantly. They can answer the call with a mouse click.

Their face will fill your screen. The image your webcam is transmitting will be in a small box at the corner of your screen. That's so you can see the video you're sending, and adjust where the camera is pointing, if necessary.

You Can Choose Standby

If they don't have Skype running in the background, or choose not to answer, you'll get a message that says there was no answer. If you want to be constantly available for others to call you on Skype, you should choose the option of launching Skype each time you turn on your computer.

If you've made all the right settings, you and the person on your screen can carry on a conversation that's sorta like being in the same room with each other. For as long as you like. Absolutely free. This is how troops stationed overseas stay in touch with their families. Truly astounding technology.

Check Skype's Drain

When it's running in the background, Skype uses three percent of my computer's available RAM. If you want to check how many resources it's using on your Windows computer when Skype is minimized, hold down the CTRL and ALT keys, then touch DELETE.

The Task Manager window will pop up. Click the PROCESSES tab. It will show how hard your CPU is working, and how much RAM is being used. With the Task Manager window still in view, close Skype and note how that affects both CPU and RAM resources.

Checking Resources On an Apple

On an Apple computer, go to APPLICATIONS, then UTILITIES, then ACTIVITY MONITOR to see how your webcam program is affecting RAM and CPU resources when it's running.

There are also a number of small programs (sometimes called "widgets") for both Windows and Apple machines that will give you more detailed information on how a program is using your system's resources. Use a search engine to find these widgets and download them.

Other Video Calling Programs

There are other video calling programs like Skype. Apple's version is Face Time. But because Skype was the pioneer in this field, it has the most users. So most of your interviews will probably use Skype. Instead of connecting through a telephone line, you're using the Internet as the connection route.

After you've had some experience with Skype, you might want to try other programs. Some may work better with your equipment.

But no matter which system you use, the people at both ends of the conversation must be using the same program.

Webcam Placement

If your webcam is perched on top of your desktop monitor, it's probably looking down its nose at you. Laptop webcams at the top of the screen frame will usually be looking up your nostrils. I'll give you ideas for adjusting the webcam height.

In normal conversations, we expect to have eye contact with the other person. That's one reason webcam interviews often look strange. When you make eye contact with the image of the person on your monitor screen, it appears to that person that you're looking up or down, not at them.

Suspicious Eye Contact

If you're not making eye contact, we suspect you're not being honest. More about that in the *On-Camera Skills* chapter.

If the conversation takes place at a party and the other person has a wandering eye, we think they're searching for someone else who's more attractive or less boring.

If you're looking down at my chest (as it appears, if the webcam is too high) I wonder if I spilled something on my shirt. A woman wonders if you're captivated by her cleavage.

Eye Level is Ideal

Ideally, the webcam should be at eye level. So if it's sitting on top of your monitor, you may need to change the height of the webcam or your chair. But that still won't solve the eye contact issue.

A better idea - buy a small tripod and put the webcam in front of the monitor.

Talking to the Webcam

In most webcam interviews you need to talk to the webcam. (See exceptions in *On-Camera Skills*) If you're looking into the lens, at the other end of the line it appears that you're making direct eye contact.

Adjust the tripod height so the lens of the webcam is at the eye level of the person onscreen that you're talking to. You don't really need to see their eyes.

The webcam and tripod may block most of the other person's face, but you'll still be able to see the body English of the person you're talking to

Another idea - if you don't have a tripod, place the webcam at eye level on something else. A stack of books will work. So will clipping the mike to a framed desktop photograph that's the right height. Either of these, however, will block a major portion of the screen. A cheap tripod works better. It can be adjusted to exactly the right height you need.

Beside the Monitor

You can also place the webcam on just about anything beside the monitor. But you'll lose the illusion of direct eye contact. I find it difficult to look at the webcam placed beside the screen and then use my peripheral vision to monitor the facial expressions and body English of the person I'm talking to. I feel less connected to them during the conversation.

My peripheral vision above and below where I'm focusing is much better than my peripheral vision on either side. You'll have to experiment to see which works best for you. Either takes practice.

More about eye contact and how to relate to the camera in the *On-Camera Skills* chapter.

How Far Away?

If you're too close to the camera, there may be some unusual - sometimes comical - distortion of your face. Your nose can grow and appear to be pressed against the lens.

Here's where a zoom lens makes a higher-quality camera a bargain. You can sit farther away to avoid the close-up distortion, and zoom in so you still fill the camera frame.

The Distance Dilemma

If you're too far away, though, that can really degrade the sound of your voice. Even with the special design of built-in webcam mikes.

Test it. If your voice doesn't sound right, try a mike that's closer to your mouth. Some very good $10 mikes can sit on the edge of the desk, in front of your keyboard.

The best solution is a clip-on mike. The kind you see TV anchor people wearing. It will always be close to your mouth. They're available now for about $30, and the quality of the sound they produce at that price point is surprisingly good.

Mike and Speaker Placement

Also be aware that the placement of the mike, in relation to your speakers, can cause audio feedback. This is especially true if your speakers and the webcam are both built into the monitor.

If you use external speakers, put them at the back edge of your desk. They'll be much less likely there to cause feedback.

Don't forget that a crying baby, a barking dog, or a ringing telephone can be a major distraction during a webcam interview.

The dog and the ringing phone can be easily fixed. The crying baby is more difficult.

Lighting & Background

Most ceiling lights put your eyes in deep shadow. It's important that we see your eyes. Television stations spend thousands of dollars to hire experts who fine-tune the lighting in their studios.

Lighting makes a huge difference in how we perceive the person on camera.

Window Disadvantages

If your desk is near a window, placing the monitor so the window is behind it will use the light coming through the window to light your face. But ONLY during daylight hours.

And you probably don't want to keep your monitor in that position all the time. Strong backlight makes it very hard to see what's on a computer monitor.

Auxiliary Lights

A better solution is one or two auxiliary lights that you'll use only for webcam interviews. Portrait photographers consider light from several directions absolutely essential if the photo is going to flatter their subject.

Almost any lights will work. They don't have to be very bright or costly. Webcams are designed to work with normal indoor lighting.

Utility lights they sell at hardware stores (right) are a great solution. They're about $10 each. They have a reflector, a push-button switch, and they come with a spring-loaded clip that makes them easy to position.

I prefer LED bulbs for this kind of fixture. They won't get hot, and they come in several colors, to match the existing lighting in the room.

White Balance

However you light the webcam interview shot, what photographers call "white balance" is critical. Daylight is much bluer than incandescent lights. Fluorescent lights are closer to daylight, but they come in several varieties.

If you use LED bulbs in auxiliary fixtures, they also come in a variety of colors. If the other lights in the room are standard incandescents, use a warm white LED. If the existing lights are fluorescents, use an LED that matches. Daylight LEDs will probably do it, but be aware that different brands labeled "daylight" vary greatly. You'll have to experiment.

The White Paper Test

Try not to mix different colors of light in the same room. To help your webcam transmit more accurate color, hold a white sheet of paper near the webcam so the paper fills the entire screen.

Then move the paper away and this can help the webcam adjusted so the color is more natural. This will work with some webcams, not with others.

Better webcams will have a setup function to let you tweak the color balance, just as you do with a TV set. When your lights are in place, you can fine-tune the color balance of your webcam.

Test Your Tuning

Test your color balance tuning by putting a white sheet of paper under your chin, so you see both your face and the paper. This can sometimes help a webcam with automatic white balancing. Does the paper appear to be truly white?

Make a test recording and then hold the paper next to the monitor so you can see if what's on screen is the same white you recorded. If not, do some more tuning.

Beware the tiny LED indicator in some webcams that tell you the camera is turned on. They're usually red or blue, and may be bright enough to make your face that same shade of red or blue. If it changes your color balance, put a piece of opaque tape over the LED indicator.

Here are some other ideas on how to light your set:

Bounce Lighting

If your ceiling is white, point a light at a spot on the ceiling above where you'll be sitting, just a little in front of directly overhead. This is called "bounce lighting." The farther the light is from the ceiling, the more it spreads.

Try moving the light higher and lower to see how that affects what you see on camera. The soft, diffused light bounced off the ceiling looks like ordinary room lighting.

Raccoon Eyes

Because bounced light is coming from directly overhead, it can create shadows under your eyebrows. Photographers call it "raccoon eyes."

To fix that, bounce a second light off the wall behind the webcam, a little to one side. IF the wall is white.

If it's not, tape some white paper or poster board to the wall, and place the second light close to it. This bounce light will fill in the shadows the overhead light creates, and put a glint in your eyes.

A Very Small Fill Light

A small light can also be the fill that removes the shadows under your eyes. Sometimes a bulb no brighter than a flashlight will do the trick. A window behind the webcam will do the same thing during daylight hours.

To light like a pro, use a third light in a far corner of the room behind you, very high, and out of camera range. It should not be very bright.

This will give a live, third dimensional look to the shot. If possible, adjust the brightness of the lights so you're well-lit and the background is fairly dark.

Brighter Looks Sharper

The brightness of your lighting will affect the F-stop or aperture of the camera. Aperture means the size of the hole that lets light into the camera. If the light is bright, the aperture gets smaller, just like the iris in the human eye.

Depth of Field

At this smaller aperture, the "depth of field" is larger. Depth of field is the distance at which objects in the video appear to be sharply in focus. With bright lighting and a very small aperture, *everything* in the entire room will be in sharp focus.

If the lighting is dim, the aperture gets bigger, and the depth of field decreases. Only the area from about one to three feet away from the camera may be in sharp focus. To the human eye, everything on-screen will seem less sharp.

Internet Tutorials

For more lighting ideas, search "portrait lighting" on the Internet. At many websites, the pros show the techniques they use to make people more attractive than they are in real life.

With a webcam, you get to see what you look and sound like. Make some test recordings and play them back. Adjust the position and brightness of the lights until you're happy with them.

Dimmers Create Orange Light

If you use a dimmer on a light, be aware that the light will become more orange as the brightness decreases. Instead of a dimmer, try bulbs of different wattages.

Some of the light should be stronger, some more subtle. Try a white umbrella or poster board to bounce light from different directions.

Be careful with the heat incandescent and halogen lights produce. Some very quickly get hot enough to set fabric or paper on fire. LED lights produce no heat. Their cool temperatures and the variety of color choices make them ideal for webcam auxiliary lighting.

The Background

This can be the most difficult task if you're setting up your webcam for interviews from your home or office. Should the background be plain or busy?

Lawyers and judges like to have a bookcase full of books behind them. It suggests they've read all of them, and are therefore true experts.

In the early days of TV news, the wall behind the anchors was blank, or looked like a window to the city where the broadcast originated.

Behind the TV Anchors

More recently, the consultants have added busy backgrounds. At some stations, we see a working newsroom behind TV anchors, with staff at keyboards and computer monitors. Or hurrying copy from one desk to another. Other setups use sculpted backgrounds in constant motion.

The newsroom in the background suggests that the anchor is the leader of a dedicated, hard-working team. And that the anchor is directly connected to the people and systems that are so diligently gathering the news.

From working in TV news for many years, I'll tell you a secret. That may not be true. The large egos of some anchors keep them psychologically separated from the peasants in the newsroom.

White House Standups

Did you ever wonder why network TV correspondents do their standups in front of the White House?

The networks have studios a few blocks away that are air conditioned, sound insulated, and well-lit.

TV Studios Would Be Easier

The studios would be a much better place for high-quality video. During the winter, it gets dark before the nightly network news at 6:30 pm (EST).

The shot on the White House lawn requires lighting. Sometimes, it's snowing. It can be noisy, and there are often people walking in the background.

But they do their standups there because having the White House in the background delivers a subliminal message. It makes the viewer believe the correspondents have been inside all day, and now they're going to tell us exactly what's going on in there.

The right background lends authority to what you say.

Subliminal Messages

As a media consultant, I tell people who work in medicine to find a spot for TV news interviews that clearly shows something to do with their profession in the background.

Like lab equipment, or personal trainers working with patients who are in rehab.

Bankers who are going to be interviewed about home mortgages should suggest to the TV news photographer that they do the interview on a street lined with "For Sale" signs.

Or in a subdivision where construction is underway. It reinforces the idea that the banker is an expert on housing loans.

What's Your Background Message?

Few of us have offices where the background will give that kind of positive reinforcement. In fact, most webcams in an office (especially a home office) will show a distracting pile of clutter.

Make It Simple

If the background can't help with the impression you'd like to give, make it as plain as possible. Like a blank wall.

The surface on the walls of cubicles in large offices are often covered with a carpet-like material that is ideal.

Whatever you choose should have a matte surface. Nothing to create reflections.

A Fabric Backdrop

A lightweight blanket can make an easy, inexpensive backdrop. They come in all sorts of colors. Two yards of terry-cloth material from a fabric store will also work. A twin-sized sheet is about the right size, but it's difficult to use because the wrinkles will show.

A dark color will usually work best. More about color in a moment. Other ideas to fill the space behind you in the webcam shot:

- An inflatable mattress sitting on end and covered by your fabric can be propped against a chair to make an easy, portable backdrop.

- If one side of the mattress is flocked, and the color is right, you might even be able to use that side of the mattress without the fabric.

- If you work in a cubicle, the fabric can be draped over the wall behind you.

- If your desk is in the right place, the fabric can be clipped to the bracket that holds vertical blinds behind you. Blinds or drapes can also be the plain backdrop.

Make An Inexpensive Frame

It's easy to make an inexpensive frame with PVC pipe that will hold your fabric. It can be disassembled when it's not in use for easy storage. See *Build a Backdrop Frame* (Page 99) for illustrated instructions on how to make one.

The farther away the backdrop, the better - for shadows, as well as camera focus. In an ideal world, you'll be in sharp focus and the backdrop will be fuzzy.

Most webcams are completely automatic, in terms of exposure. You don't have the ability to change the camera aperture.

Lighting/Depth of Field Conflict

So with an automatic camera, there is a conflict between good lighting and depth of field. The brighter the light, the smaller the aperture.

The smaller the aperture, the greater the depth of field in which everything will be in sharp focus.

If we're distracted by something in the background, you didn't do a very good job in your setup. Nothing should detract from you and your message.

Color and Automatic Exposure

With automatic exposure, the camera measures the lightness and darkness of everything in the entire shot and comes up with an average that sets the aperture.

If you have a white wall or fabric as the backdrop, the camera reacts the way your eye would - Wow! It's bright in here! - and the aperture stops down. The camera shot makes it look like you've turned down the lights in the room. The smaller aperture changes depth of field. Everything in the room will be sharply in focus.

A dark background has the opposite effect. The camera thinks - Wow! Its dark in here! - and the aperture opens up. Your face can look washed out, like you're caught in a powerful spotlight. The larger aperture will make the background fuzzy.

Tailored Exposure

So the goal is to set up a background that makes the webcam auto exposure just right for your complexion.

A test question - If you have very dark skin, should the background be light or dark? The answer is counter-intuitive.

The correct answer: Dark. The webcam's measure of light and darkness in the entire frame will give you a wider aperture and light your face better than it would with a light background. With a light background, the details of your face can be almost invisible.

If you're extremely pale, a light background can make it look like you have a healthy tan.

Testing to Make it Right

There is no magic formula. The only way to find out what's right for you is to test different shades of light and dark until you find the right one.

Color itself is not that important for exposure. It is *lightness* and *darkness* that make the difference.

More about color and the clothes to wear in the *On-Camera Skills* chapter.

The Job Interview

Job interviews by webcam are becoming more and more common.

The *On-Camera Skills* chapter is focused on interviews for TV news stories. You should read that chapter, too, because a lot of the same skills apply to both kinds of interviews. I didn't want to repeat too much in the two chapters.

Most Important: Sincerity

Nothing works better on camera than sincerity. Most people fall short because they don't know how to be sincere to a camera. The trick is to imagine that the camera is a real person. Someone you know and like. Someone you feel comfortable with.

I remember watching the British actor Michael Caine being interviewed on *The Today Show*. The BBC was filming a series of documentaries called "Masters of Their Craft." Caine had been chosen as a master of the acting craft.

Making Love to the Camera

"How did you learn to be a master craftsman?" the interviewer asked.

"I learned how to make love to the camera," Caine responded.

"What do you mean?" he was asked.

"Watch," Caine said.

And suddenly he changed. Still the same person, but he was warmer. The voice was more intimate. He was someone you'd like to spend time with; exchange secrets with. In teaching on-camera skills I use the same concept with my clients.

Imagine that the person you're talking to is the love of your life, I tell them. You're on your first date. He or she is across the table in a restaurant. Turn on your charm. You want that person sitting across from you to like you. Believe you. Trust you.

Job Interviews Are a First Date

In many ways, job interviews *are* a first date. Many of the same goals and ideas apply. You need to relax and let the person at the other end of the Skype connection see you at your best. Your most sincere.

Tell them about the things you love. The things you hate. The things you do well. Your hopes. Your dreams. Your passions. What excites you.

Why People Get Hired

If you're sincere, and it shows, that's what makes people like you. Fall in love with you. And hire you.

I sometimes say to clients that I'm coaching: "You're not connecting to me. I feel like there's a pane of glass between us. You've got to figure out how to open that window. Only you can do that. It happens inside your head."

Another suggestion I make is to imagine you're having a drink with me. Don't talk company public relations brochure language.

Tell me what you really think. What you're really concerned about. What you hope to accomplish. It's after work. We've left the office and gone to a bar to unwind.

Sometimes, I put a glass in their hand, to help with their mind-set. Have another drink, I say, and TALK to me.

"On the Side of God & the Angels"

I also believe in mantras to help you communicate better. I tell clients who are preparing for court testimony to repeat over and over on the way to the courthouse:

"I am on the side of God and the angels. I am going to speak truth today to bring light and justice to the world."

Learning to Say It Quickly

Most of us on that first date with the love of our life talked for hours. By comparison, a job interview is very short. So you need to learn how to summarize.

The ultimate news media skill is to learn how to tell the history of the human race in one sentence, without taking breath.

The Elevator Speech

In a job interview, you MUST summarize. It's been called "the elevator speech." Tell me what I need to know in the time it takes the elevator to go from one floor to the next.

If the interviewer is interested in your summary, they'll ask a follow-up question. You'll be given more time to expand your thoughts.

Record and Study Your Answers

There are a number of standard questions most job interviewers ask. You should practice your answers, record them with your webcam, and study the replay very carefully.

You may record your answer a dozen times before you're happy with it. Answers to questions like:

Questions They're Likely to Ask

- Why should we hire you?
- What are your best skills?
- What are your weaknesses?
- Where do you see yourself in the next five or 10 years?
- How easy are you to work with?
- How well do you perform under pressure?
- Are you a team player?
- How soon could you come to work if we hired you?
- Why did you leave your last job ... or
- Why do you want to leave your present job?
- What do you consider your greatest accomplishment?
- What was your worst failure?
- What did you learn from your mistakes?
- If you disagree with the boss, will you say so?

Questions They Can't Ask

There are also questions they can't ask. Employers are forbidden to discriminate in hiring because of your:

- Race or nationality
- Age
- Religion
- Marital status
- Health and physical disabilities

Disguising Forbidden Questions

But they'd still like to know some of those things. So they'll get around the rules by asking disguised questions like:

- How fluent are you in Spanish?
- Have you set an age at which you'd like to retire?
- Would you be willing to work on holidays?
- Would you be able to travel a lot if we hire you?

They Can't Ask, But You Can Tell

So work into your interview things like:

- On weekends, I run at least five miles to stay in shape
- English is my first language, but I do pretty well in Spanish and French
- My friends say I look younger than I am, but I've got 10 years' experience since I received my master's degree from M.I.T.
- I'm single, and don't have a serious relationship right now, so I can hit the road tomorrow if you need me to be somewhere
- I'm accustomed to long hours, and since I don't have any family obligations, I'm available for assignments on weekends and holidays

Dealing with Interview Stress

In *On-Camera Skills* I write about the stage fright that often accompanies a TV interview. A job interview can be even more stressful, because so much may be riding on your being hired.

Before the Interview

Physical exercise like running or swimming before the interview can help. Stay away from stimulants and alcohol. Drinks with caffeine can not only make you feel wired, they dry out your throat. Your voice can sound fuzzy, or you'll need to frequently clear your throat. Milk can also affect your voice.

Get Your Head in the Right Place

Repeat a mantra in your head before the interview. Something like:

- I'm exactly the person they're looking for.

- I've never been more qualified for anything than I am for this job.

Have a conversation with a friend who's upbeat and encouraging. Having someone on your side will make the interview less intimidating.

Do something you really enjoy, like playing a musical instrument or a video game. Have information on your desk within easy reach that can help if you forget something.

Scheduling the Interview

If you're sharper in the morning, or drowsy after lunch, schedule the webcam interview when you'll be at your best. Have a glass of water on your desk, in case your mouth gets dry.

What to Wear

Dress the way the employees at this company do when they're working. That means maybe a dress shirt and tie, if you're a man, but no coat. Be sure to read how clothing and jewelry are critical to the impressions women make, in the chapter *On-Camera Skills*.

Fine Lines You Need to Understand

In the on-camera interview, there are fine lines that can be drawn that will dramatically affect how you're perceived. And the only way you can know where those lines are - for you - is to practice with your webcam and study the replay.

The traits below are GOOD/BAD. The first is usually considered good by most employers - but if you cross the line and overplay them, you can give a bad impression. There is often a very thin line distinguishing them. It can be a very slight inflection in your voice, facial expression or body English. Here's a list of those kinds of traits:

Walking the Tightrope

Self-confident/Arrogant

Aggressive/Overpowering

Risk-taker/Reckless

Hard worker/Workaholic

Empathetic/Maudlin

Precise-well organized/Obsessive-compulsive

Sense of humor/Takes nothing seriously

Humble/Meek

Cool, calm/Uncaring

Decisive/Control freak

Enthusiastic/Wild and unpredictable

Careful/Wimpy and afraid of new ideas

Laugh at yourself/Self-deprecating

Creative/Unmanageable

Everybody Says That

During political campaigns, every candidate promises to cut taxes and stop government waste. We hear it so much, it no longer registers. In one ear, and out the other.

The same thing happens in job interviews.

ALL the applicants say they are the best qualified for this job, and the company will be glad they were picked.

If you do make that kind of statement, IMMEDIATELY follow it with an example, a story, the hard evidence that what you just said is true and believable. Read more about this idea in *Creating Sound Bites*.

You Must Stand Out in the Crowd

If you're going to be hired, you will have to be unusual. Memorable. A Google search for "job interviews" will return about SIX MILLION hits.

There are unlimited resources out there to help you do well. Do your homework. Know the company that's going to interview you. Work on your resumé.

Practice, Practice, Practice

For my book, *Winning With the News Media*, I created the Ten Commandments of Media Relations. One of them is: Practice, Practice, Practice. The same thing applies to job interviews. With a webcam, you have the world's greatest training tool.

Record practice interviews, with a friend who has a webcam asking the questions you know the prospective employer is going to ask. Study the replays.

And then do it again. Over and over again, until you're comfortable with the results. The process will become easier as you practice. You'll see things about yourself you were not aware of. You can change them, if you work at it.

And you'll get hired.

Be the Expert On Call

And now, the good news (I've already told you the bad news about webcam interviews).

The quality of webcam hardware and software has improved so much that if you follow the advice in the earlier chapters of this book, and learn how to use your webcam, you can transmit video and audio that is nearing broadcast quality.

Webcams Offer Unique Opportunities

That opens up an opportunity to promote your career or organization or point of view that has never before been possible.

Television news is constantly looking for experts who can analyze and offer more insight in their stories. The networks have experts under contract who do this regularly. Medical, economic, legal, military experts.

Is Your Number In Their Contact List?

I've always told my media relations clients that one of their primary goals should be to have their names and numbers in the electronic versions of the old Rolodex® system for every reporter and editor in their community.

When I was reporting for WPLG-TV in Miami, there was a stock broker who specialized in airline stocks. He was also very good at giving quick, concise interviews.

If anything happened that was connected to airlines or air travel, you could call, drive to his office, and interview him immediately.

The "Super" Billboard

Miami was a big city for airline news - gateway to Latin America - home office of several airlines - the site of some major crashes. The broker frequently appeared in those stories as an expert/analyst.

And every time one of his interviews was broadcast, his name and brokerage firm appeared on the "super" across his chest. He was a pioneer in using the technique.

Experts On TV Get Free Advertising

Here's a great example. Diane Swonk is so good at this, several networks use her as a financial expert in their news stories. She's created a small TV set in her office.

Notice the light coming from the upper left. Very professional. She's also looking slightly beside the camera, as if she's talking to a reporter there.

This kind of exposure as the expert analyst is incredibly valuable to your career and business. TV commercials are expensive. One of their primary goals is to embed brand names in the minds of viewers. As an expert, your interview does the same thing for you and your organization.

It convinces us that you know a lot about the subject. Otherwise, they wouldn't have asked your opinion. And we know you didn't buy the TV time. A news interview makes you much more believable than a commercial would.

The Local News Peg

One of the most persistent, predictable kinds of stories is a local story "pegged" to a national or international story. American editors are genetically programmed - absolutely compelled - to publish and broadcast these stories.

If America sends combat troops into a foreign country, local media MUST produce a story on whether or how local soldiers might be involved.

When a major bridge collapses, reporters all across the country write "pegged" stories about whether local bridges are safe.

When a breakthrough in cancer treatment is announced, the local TV station's audience wants to know when it will be available locally, and where.

What is News?

One of the most succinct definitions of news:

NEWS IS THE UNUSUAL.

If the headline says The Mayor Was Sober Today, it means that's unusual.

So reporters need experts to tell us how unusual the event they're writing about really is. Their stories need a little history on why today's event is so notable. And an expert who predicts what it all means is absolutely essential.

Who Qualifies as an Expert?

Experts need a lot of knowledge and experience in their field. They are much more credible if their opinions will not affect them (or their competitors) financially.

This is why college professors are interviewed so often for news stories. Their education, knowledge and arm's-length experience are a given.

If we find out they have a financial interest in the company that manufactures the product they're analyzing, their believability goes down the tubes.

The Ethics of Expertise

The expert should fully disclose anything that might even *suggest* a conflict of interest.

Medical school professors, for instance, should not provide their opinion or analysis of an experimental procedure in which they are involved, unless that is disclosed, right up front.

Law school professors should not be telling us about the court process for a current case if they are also consulting with one of the trial lawyers on jury selection in that case.

How to Become the Expert on Call

If appearing in TV news stories appeals to you, here's how to do it:

- Read EVERY WORD in this book

- Buy and set up a high-quality webcam

- Create a "set" in your office (more about that in the *Lighting and Background* chapter)

- Practice, practice, practice on camera

- Be aware of today's breaking news through the Internet or a local 24-hour newscast

- When a story appears in which your opinion or analysis would be valuable, call the news director of a local TV station immediately (tomorrow will probably be too late)

- Explain your expertise and what you could say if you were interviewed

- Tell him/her you have a high-quality webcam and could do the interview in the next 30 minutes

- If that news director is not interested, call another

- If you do the interview well, let the news director know you can be on call for any future stories that involve your expertise

Local Angle on National News

Often the story that could use your expertise is a national or international story. You may know of some local angle that local editors and reporters are not aware of.

They'd LOVE to have a locally-pegged story on the big national story. Call and suggest the story idea. Just a suggestion. Don't sell too hard. You'll make the news director suspicious.

Get Acquainted

If you've created your own webcam set and practiced until you think you're ready, let local news directors know about your expertise, your webcam equipment, and your willingness to help them flesh out future stories in your field. They'll probably want to audition you.

Don't Push to Be Paid

It's usually best to not talk too much about being paid in your first conversations with a news director. That comes later. After they've used interviews with you several times, you'll probably have a working relationship with the news director.

They may make an offer before you bring it up.

If not, ask if other experts on call for the station are paid. If none are, you might shop around at another local station.

Suggest that you'd like to be on call for quick interviews in your field with a title like "consultant" or "special correspondent." This kind of arrangement could include a written contract that pays you each time you appear.

Creating Your Set

Read the *Lighting and Background* chapter carefully. The last chapter in this book- *Build a Backdrop Frame* - shows how to make a simple frame to hold a fabric backdrop. As an expert-on-call, you might want to work on something fancier.

In virtually every community, there's a photographer whose portfolio includes pictures of the city skyline, and major institutions there.

Or you can shoot it yourself. It's easy to have a wall-sized print made.

Another idea - a large LCD monitor on the wall over your shoulder can show still photos or video.

The City Skyline as Backdrop

Either can become the backdrop for your set. TV stations often have the city skyline as the background for their anchors. If your expertise is aviation, the backdrop can be a photo of the local airport, or a plane.

A lot of Wall Street firms have sets with their logos, or a live view of the market floor in the background. Their experts do live cut-ins during the day. It builds their brand recognition.

Suggested Areas of Expertise

Here and on the following pages, I've listed areas where you might be able to contribute your expertise. Local TV news needs you and would love to have the immediacy, ease and economy of a webcam. IF you create high-quality video and audio AND you're good on camera.

COLLEGES & UNIVERSITIES - Virtually every college and university with a public relations department works at arranging interviews with professors who are experts and good on camera. The webcam makes this process much easier. The PR department should build its own webcam set and let media contacts know about it.

MEDICINE - Large hospitals and research facilities have copied the college and university model. There is a HUGE interest in everything medical. Few fields have a greater need for experts who can explain, in simple language, what the latest technology can do or what today's medical journal story means.

EDUCATION - If you have experience as a teacher, principal or school administrator, there's at least one story every week on local TV news that could use your expertise and perspective.

BANKS & INVESTMENT FIRMS - The recession of 2008 made financial news more popular than at any time since the Great Depression. There is a local news peg in this field almost every day.

REAL ESTATE - The same thing is true for everything in the real estate/housing market. New construction, sales in your area, financing statistics, comparisons with this year versus last. Endless opportunities.

ASSOCIATION ADVOCATES - Local news stories, in their effort to be fair, often need someone who can speak for another side of the issue. America has tens of thousands of associations representing every conceivable occupation and cause. If you're an officer in one of those associations, and your job is to advocate for your members, a webcam is tailor-made for your mission.

POLITICS - You'll do much better in this field if it's clear you don't ever plan to run for office. The work is seasonal - mostly during political campaigns. The political analyst's role is carved in stone at the networks. Some of them seem to put in 16-hour days telling us what all the campaign stuff means in the weeks and months before an election. And then they analyze results on election night.

THE JUSTICE SYSTEM - Former judges, lawyers and prosecutors are in demand to explain to ordinary folks what's happening in court, how the system works, and what to expect next. If you're still working, you may not able to ethically comment on any pending case. Just the court system.

TRAVEL & ACCIDENTS - A wide range of companies and professions have expertise in this area. From accident statistics to the price of gasoline and current car sales. The American Automobile Association has carved its own niche here. AAA spokespeople are always on hand before holidays to tell us how crowded the roads will be, construction areas to avoid, and where to find cheap gas.

AUTOMOBILES - If you're a master mechanic and know something about how cars are manufactured and sold, there's a slot waiting for you. Click and Clack, the Tappet Brothers became icons on National Public Radio. There are lots of other ideas waiting for this kind of knowledge to insert in local TV news stories.

AVIATION - The same thing is true for any story involving commercial or private aviation. All the TV networks have former pilots, air traffic controllers, travel agents and administrators on standby to help them explain what might have happened in today's accident, system meltdown or close call.

UTILITIES & INFRASTRUCTURE - This is another high volume story type for local TV news. When the lights or water get turned off; when roads or bridges buckle or get shut down because of the aging process, they need to know:

Why did this happen? Reporters try to explain, but most of them aren't engineers. If you have knowledge in this field, and can explain it so fifth graders can understand, you have a future in TV news.

CRIME & LAW ENFORCEMENT - Here's another great opportunity for retired police officers. EVERY newscast in America features crime stories. And they often have a puzzling element or twist. A former cop with experience behind a badge can often give great insight to the story.

THE NEWS MEDIA - As newspapers wither and die, dozens of other formats are taking their place. We are experiencing a major revolution in how America gets its news. Puzzling, unless you work - or once worked - there, and can help viewers understand what's happening, and what it means to the democracy.

This is just a small sampling of the areas where expert witnesses and analysts have huge new opportunities and a chance to make a difference - if they learn how to do it by webcam.

On-Camera Skills

In the early part of this book, I explained why webcam interviews can put you at a real disadvantage.

But if you'll follow my suggestions for setting up your webcam, you'll have a distinct advantage -

- By recording yourself, you can know what you look and sound like

- You can work to improve your skills, and

- You can rehearse a specific interview, then study the replay and hone your answers

Do You Have a Webcam?

If TV wants to interview you by webcam, a reporter or producer will usually telephone to ask if you have a webcam. If you do, and they're in a hurry, they might want to call you back on Skype immediately to record the video interview.

When TV news wants an interview, the first basic rule is:

RULE # 1 Give Yourself Time

Give yourself time to prepare before you talk.

If your pulse is racing, pause. This rule is especially critical if the reporter's call makes your adrenaline surge or pulse rate jump.

You won't think well in fight-or-flight mode. You need a little time to get back to normal. To get your thoughts together.

The quotes that people regret are usually said reflexively, in the traumatic surge of anger or shock that follows a rude surprise or sudden loss.

If you can stall for even 10 minutes, you'll do a better job of speaking for yourself or your organization.

Can I Call You Back?

So you say to the reporter or producer who's on the phone, "I'm really busy on something right now. I think I can finish it in about 15 minutes. Can I call you back then?"

Which is true. You have a lot of work to do to get ready for this interview. If that timetable works for them, get a quick grasp of what the story is about. What do they want in their interview with you? Then hang up and spend the 15 minutes getting ready.

Everything in One Sentence

Use the time to decide what you really want to say. Boil it down to one sentence you can speak without taking a breath. That one sentence will become the foundation of the interview. Other thoughts will branch out from it, but you'll want to keep coming back to it. Explaining it. Expanding it.

Repeat the Central Idea

In normal conversation, if you repeat yourself, we wonder if you're getting senile. But in a news interview (that's being recorded, not live) if you say it often enough, at least one of those quotes or sound bites that states the central idea is more likely to be used.

As a TV reporter, before a friendly interview, I would often say to my interviewee: "I may ask you the same question several times. It doesn't mean I'm not listening. That's a signal that I think you can give me a better, shorter answer. It means let's try that one again."

In normal conversation, we build up to our conclusion. We lay the groundwork first, before we get to the point. In media interviews, the process is reversed.

Always give the conclusion first. Then tell us how you got there. This takes practice. It's like telling a joke, punch line first.

Check With Staff

During that 15-minute reprieve before you make the webcam connection, check with your staff. "A reporter just called. The story they're pursuing caught me completely by surprise. Is there something I should know?"

The delay rule isn't necessary if the reporter's request is for simple information that poses no threat. But if you react viscerally, buy some time.

If the interview is critical to you or your organization, do it in person, if possible. Forget the webcam. It's much easier for you to get a handle on the reporter and the story angle if you're really face-to-face. Personalities sometimes don't transmit accurately if the conversation is done electronically.

Make Sure It IS a Reporter

If you don't recognize the name or voice of the reporter on the phone and the story is sensitive, use the delay tactic. Before you hook up by webcam, make sure the call is legitimate.

The callback number the caller gave you may bypass the switchboard. So call the TV station or network's listed number and ask for the person who requested the interview.

Private detectives, insurance investigators, political opponents and business competitors sometimes pose as journalists. They'd love to catch you by surprise on video.

Ambushes by Webcam

If they know you always have Skype running in the background, you can be the victim of a webcam ambush - a surprise, instant video interview. If it's a TV reporter or producer, FCC regulations require them to tell you you're on the air.

Once you've agreed to be interviewed by webcam, and after you've done your homework, the next rule is:

RULE # 2 - The Pre-Interview-Interview

Conduct what I call a pre-interview-interview. From the first contact, where you arranged to delay the interview for a few minutes, you know generally what the story is about. When you call back, or when the webcam connection is made, expand that inquiry. Weave it into the social chat that begins most conversations.

Getting Acquainted

If you understand what the reporter is after, you can save a lot of time and anxiety. In this get-acquainted conversation, try to learn some basics:

- What exactly is the story assignment, and who thought it up?

- When will the story run, and what is the deadline for finishing it?

- How much time will the story be given?

- Who else has the reporter interviewed?

- Has any other research been done?

- How much knowledge does this reporter seem to have on this subject, and what kind of preconceptions?

- How intelligent and experienced does the reporter seem to be?

What is the Story About?

This is a very important thing you need to know, so you can judge whether the reporter is working on a preconceived concept that may be misguided. If that's the case, you'll have to work very hard to swing the story in another direction.

Particularly if the misconception came from the reporter's assignment editor or news director. The reporter doesn't want to tell the boss the story idea was stupid. You'll have to work very hard to convince the reporter the boss' story concept should be abandoned.

Are They Here To Hurt You?

Before the real interview begins, you should have a good idea about whether the reporter will try to gut you, or simply needs your sound bites to fill out the story – to give it authority and credibility.

Young, inexperienced reporters are rarely given tough investigative assignments. If not done right, those stories can bring lawsuits. If the reporter seems very sharp, and seems to know a lot about the subject, that can be a warning flag.

As an investigative reporter, the interview with my target was my last stop before I wrote the script. I wanted to know as much as possible before the interview, so I'd know which questions to ask, and whether my target was lying.

The Play Dumb Con

Good investigative reporters can also con you into believing they're dumb and innocent, so you'll talk more freely. They'll respond with "no kidding?" or "really!" to things they already know. That makes you want to tell them more.

You may learn in the pre-interview interview that you need to gather some more written information to help you recall exact facts and figures.

A Great Opportunity

If you discover the reporter knows very little about the subject matter, you have a great opportunity to steer the story your way. The way you structure the pre-interview conversation can strongly influence the questions when the real interview begins.

The interview may simply repeat the earlier conversation. That's all the new, inexperienced reporter knows to ask.

If the Reporter Offers, Take It

Many new reporters, uncomfortable with their knowledge and skill, may even tell you in advance exactly what they're going to ask. If they make the offer, take it.

Remember: EVERYTHING is recorded. Avoid any asides that could easily become the story or change the way it's written. Anything you do or say can come back to haunt you.

Why Was That In the Story?

Avoid the temptation to educate the reporter too much. An inexperienced reporter may not be able to pick out the most important things you said.

"Why was that in the story?" you'll think when it's broadcast. Because you gave the information to the reporter. So stick to the topic and don't wander around. This gives you much more control of what's eventually on the air.

It is considered unethical for a reporter to tell you exactly what the questions will be. The interview is supposed to be a spontaneous conversation. To rehearse either questions or answers is staging. But there is a fine line here.

Most reporters consider it proper to tell you the subject they're covering and broad areas they want to explore in the interview. Find out as much as you can.

Be aware that the reporter will also be sizing you up. The impression you give in those first few minutes after you connect can be critical to the questions you'll be asked, and the slant on the story.

Have Your Staff Handy

For stories that involve a lot of numbers or complicated, technical details, it's a good idea to have your staff experts nearby. They can hand you notes or documents when you grope for the right number.

You can ask them to fetch details the reporter needs for the story. When you get the information you need, the reporter can re-ask the question. Having a friend in your corner may also make you feel more at ease and less threatened.

Don't Cram

For the interview, you don't need to do a lot of cramming. If you, the expert, can't remember, how do you expect viewers to retain what you say? The reporter will not use many numbers in a sound bite you say on camera.

Go over the numbers before, or after, the interview. Most people can't absorb spoken statistics. They do remember analogies and perspective.

This is what we'll remember if you say in the interview:

"The money we'll spend this year treating this disease would buy everybody in the state a new Lexus."

Provide Graphs & Charts

If the audience is to retain numbers, the story will greatly benefit if it has graphs and charts that put them in perspective.

Seeing the numbers on the screen while they are spoken doubles viewer retention.

Most reporters in major cities would not think of printing or broadcasting a news release exactly as you wrote it. But they will often use your graphs or charts with no editing whatever. Virtually every computer word processing program has graph and charting capability.

Your providing graphics will help the story immensely.

Tell the reporter while you're connected by webcam that you have the graphics and can attach them to an e-mail after you hang up, if that would be helpful.

Interview Eye Contact

If the reporter were in the room with you, videotaping an interview, you'd talk to the reporter, not the camera. The camera is just listening to the conversation.

The camera doesn't ask questions. The reporter does. So if you answer into the camera, the audience reacts:

The reporter asked the question - why are you giving me the answer?

A Different Perspective

Webcam interviews have a completely different perspective. Here, you're talking to the reporter, but eye contact will depend on how the interview is going to be used.

Ask, before you begin, where they would like you to look.

If the anchor is talking to someone live, the audience knows the setup and the person being interviewed normally talks to the camera. The audience watches the interaction.

The custom is no longer rigid. Some experts are being told in their remote interviews (where the reporter was not with them when it was recorded) to look slightly to one side.

In that way, it will appear that they took part in a normal conversation, while the camera eavesdropped.

Where Do You Want Me to Look?

So ask them where they want you to look. If you don't talk to the webcam, you'll need to look slightly to one side. Keep eye contact with one edge of your monitor. They may have a choice between left or right.

Wherever they tell you to look, if your eyes get weary, take a break by looking down at your desk for a moment. As if you were in deep thought.

No Gazing Into Space

If you look off into space while you're talking or thinking about the question, the audience tends to believe you're making up the answer. That you're not being honest.

That's why placement of the webcam (learn more in the *Webcam Placement* chapter) is so critical.

If the webcam is too high, it appears at the other end that you're being interviewed by a giant, and have to look up to maintain eye contact.

Giants and Midgets

If the webcam is too low, it appears that you're the giant, looking down at this reporter who must be about four feet tall. If the webcam placement is badly done, your face will be distorted.

Try not to blink too much. That can also be interpreted as a sign of stress or deception.

Office Chair Hazards

Office chairs are a real hazard. You'll want to rock. Stress makes you twist back and forth while you rock. The chairs sometimes squeak. The viewer gets seasick as you bob up and down on screen.

A non-rocking office chair with a hydraulic lift is ideal. You can position it so the webcam is at your eye level. You can put it back to your normal working level when the interview is over.

Don't Lean Back

Sit up straight and don't lean back in the chair. Leaning back changes your body English. You tell us, without words, that you're not very enthusiastic about what you're saying.

Or that you're trying to put as much distance as you can between you and the person at the other end of the connection.

Television anchors are taught to sit this way. It may seem, at first, a little strange. You move your butt to the edge of the chair. This changes your posture. It straightens the spine. You appear to be alert and self-confident. Your words have more authority. You find that your arms on the table are lighter. It's easier to use gestures as you speak.

Some Examples

Here's *CBS This Morning* anchor Norah O'Donnell (below) in a classic anchor sitting posture. It may seem awkward at

first. When I sit this way, I put one leg out to steady myself.

It feels like I may fall off the chair if I don't. Try it.

Everyone is different. Once you master this technique, you can do it for hours and be comfortable. It's also great if you're a witness in court, appearing on a panel, or testifying before a legislative committee.

And here's a guest on that same show, who obviously has had some on-camera training.

If you MUST use a swivel chair that rocks, crank the spring tension as tight as it will go to make the back of chair as rigid as possible.

Remember not to swivel.

Take Your Time

During the interview (unless it's being broadcast live) take your time. If you start a sentence that gets tangled and confused, start again. That's what editing is for.

TV reporters also fluff their lines when they're videotaping and have to repeat them to get it right. They understand, and will almost always let you go back and start again.

If you don't understand the question, say so. If you're nervous and your mouth is dry, stop for a drink of water. Keep thinking of the living room and the friend or neighbor you im-

agine you're talking to. That will help relieve the nervous-
ness.

Take More Control

Once the interview starts, most people give up all control of
their lives to the reporter. Don't do that. Take more control.
You can say things like:

You know, I gave you an answer several minutes ago that
took me much too long to get to the point. If you'll ask me
that same question again, I think I can give you a better,
shorter answer. OR

I just realized I made a mistake when I answered one of
your questions. What I said was not completely accurate.
Let's go back over that again. I'll get it right this time.

Short and Simple

Try to talk in short, simple sentences. Lawyers and professors have a tendency to speak in outlined, organized form -
firstly, secondly, thirdly - or to label their points A, B and C.

If the reporter is only interested in your third point, and
you've run the words together, they may not be able to edit
out "thirdly." That entire thought may be discarded in the editing process.

Other Editing Nightmares

Other common phrases like "first of all" and "as I said earlier"
can create editing nightmares. There may not be enough
time in a news story to let you say it twice, or to include your
"first of all" point.

If you drop "as I said earlier" in the middle of a sentence, the
entire sentence may have to be dumped.

Avoid dating the interview. If you say something happened
yesterday, the story may not be used until tomorrow. By then
whatever happened was the day before yesterday.

Like Talking to a Jury

Some of the best on-camera interviews are with trial lawyers
who've spent their entire careers summing up complicated
cases for jurors. They keep it short and simple, conversa-

tional and colorful. They're good at one-sentence conclusions jurors will remember and repeat to each other in the jury room.

For the main point, they let their feelings show. Jurors are very much like those people sitting in front of the television set after a hard day's work. They're easily bored. They want it simple. They want it interesting. They want to know what it was really like to be there. How did it feel?

Beware Uhh, Ahh, You Know

It is critical that you listen to yourself speak for several minutes to learn how often you pause and say Uhh or Ahh. The entire country in recent years inserts "you know" in every other phrase. Sometimes two or three times in the same sentence.

TERRIBLE. And a very difficult habit to break.

Drop the Parentheticals

Any kind of parenthetical thought can make a sentence too long for television news. Example - a politician says:

"I've come to believe, as most of my constituents do, if they've had any experience with firearms, that every person in this country has the God-given right to own a gun."

It can be edited much easier if the politician says:

"I believe every person in this country has the God-given right to own a gun. (Pause for possible edit point) I'm sure most of my constituents who have any experience with firearms feel the same way I do."

With this version, the reporter can use either sentence, or both. They can also be separated to use in different parts of the story.

Anticipate the Why

Another technique that can help the editing process:

QUESTION: Then you will not vote, Senator, to outlaw Saturday Night Specials?

ANSWER: No.

QUESTION: Why?

ANSWER: The Saturday Night Special is a phony issue.

QUESTION: Why do you say that?

ANSWER: Most police officers, and most store clerks, are killed with expensive weapons. Why should the poor homeowner be denied a weapon he can afford to protect himself and his family?

If you give a "Yes" or "No" answer, it will almost always be followed by "Why?" Anticipate the why, and if you repeat the question as part of your answer, it saves valuable response time between questions and answers.

Another Way to Do It Quickly

This answer will enable the reporter to cram the entire response into about two-thirds as much time:

QUESTION: Then you will not vote, Senator, to outlaw Saturday Night Specials?

ANSWER: I will never vote to outlaw Saturday Night Specials. They're a phony issue. Most police officers ... etc.

Incorporating the question into your answer allows the reporter to drop the sound bite into the story without having to set up what you were asked.

Show Me While You Tell Me

What the audience sees, if you're genuine, may communicate more than what they hear. Years ago, advertising agencies learned how to use visual suggestions in print.

A lot can be said in a picture that doesn't require words. Because of television's time limitations, that technique has become a science.

The real message is visual, not verbal. And it is usually more powerful than words.

How TV Commercials Use Visuals

Luxury car commercials tell us about the wonderful engineering or handling of the automobile. But the more effective message is what we see.

The driver is pulling up to a home that cost several million dollars. Or sliding behind the wheel at the country club. Or at the airport, with a corporate jet in the background.

And, of course, there is a trophy wife or husband in the passenger seat. The key visual message: If you're rich, sophisticated, influential, sexually attractive, you'll buy this car.

Visual Shorthand

Politicians have learned to use the same kind of visual symbolism to communicate with their constituents. After a flood or earthquake, it is now a tribal ritual for the governor - dressed in fatigues and combat boots - to survey the damage from a National Guard helicopter.

Is that really necessary? Can't governors get reports from experts who are better equipped to assess the damage?

Yes, but we've come to expect a personal visit. If we don't see the governor, the president or the vice president at the scene of a major disaster, we think they don't care.

This used to be called a "photo opportunity." The new word for it is "optics."

More Important Than What You Say

I have done a lot of law enforcement training. Chiefs and sheriffs worry about what they will say the day an officer is killed in the line of duty.

I tell them I'm much more concerned about what the public will SEE them doing. A picture is worth a thousand words. Maybe a million.

You need to be seen at the scene, I tell them. You know TV cameras will be at the hospital, at the officer's home. And if you're not at the funeral, kiss your job good-bye. Being there speaks volumes. Not being there also delivers a powerful message.

Clothing Messages

The clothes you wear are part of the visual shorthand. When he was president, Jimmy Carter liked to be interviewed in a plaid shirt and sweater.

To enhance his "just plain folks" image, Carter often carried a piece of luggage when he was embarking from a plane or helicopter - even though a small army of aides and Secret Service agents were there, empty-handed. Richard Nixon wanted to suggest a more regal kind of presidency. You sometimes wondered if he slept in a coat and tie.

Barack Obama was the master of knowing when to get rid of his coat, and sometimes his tie. It depends on the time and place where you'll be filmed.

> (An aside - Almost nobody shoots film any more. The verb has taken on the meaning of any video which is shot. Partly because there are so many different recording media now.)

Coats and Ties

A CEO wearing his coat and tie behind an immaculate desk tells us, subliminally, that he is a figurehead who is aloof, unfamiliar with his employees, and rarely gets involved in the nuts and bolts of running the company. A paper shuffler.

Let's design another scenario. The desktop has some papers scattered on it, with a computer at one side. The CEO has his coat off, tie loose, sleeves rolled up. The impression changes. He seems hands-on, hard-working, personally involved.

Learn From Candidates

You can learn a lot from presidential candidates. They have very high-priced consultants who tell them what to wear. During his 2008 and 2012 campaigns, Barack Obama usually appeared with a dress shirt, no coat, no tie.

After he was elected, he did the same thing when he went on the road to sell his issues. But for recorded messages from the Oval Office, he wore a coat and tie.

As this is being written, Donald Trump does not seem yet to have figured this out.

I suggest to my clients that if they normally come to work in business clothes, they should also keep some more casual clothes at the office, for certain unexpected interviews.

There is now a demeaning term for men who wear coats and ties - "the suits." Most Americans no longer dress like that at work. The message you deliver in that kind of clothing may be that you're old, out-of-date, and uninvolved in the real work your organization does.

What Should Women Wear?

Women's clothing is much more complex. There are so many more choices. The standard coat and tie for men is a sort of uniform. As both a public official and candidate, Hillary Clinton decided to wear a pant suit, no matter what the occasion.

It was partly to hide the weight she gained as she aged. But after awhile, her clothing reminded me of the uniforms Asian leaders adopted. If she had asked for my advice (she didn't) I would have suggested that her failure to wear different styles might make some people suspect she was inflexible in her thinking or personality.

More Suggestions for Women

This may seem obvious, but wear something that fits. It shouldn't sag or bag. Clothes that are too tight, or tug at your waist or chest, really stand out and catch the viewers' attention.

Don't wear something that's too big, either. The color of clothes, or the style, matters less than how it fits.

That said, don't wear colors that are too loud or bright. They distract. If you have time to choose, select items that complement your face color.

Makeup Ideas

Make sure lipstick and blush match and don't clash. For most women, matte finish lipstick works better than gloss. Be sure to use powder on any spots that tend to be shiny.

Use light-colored eye shadow directly over your lids, darker colors in the lid crease, light skin color tones under the eyebrows, and apply moderate to heavy eyeliner and mascara.

Do a dress rehearsal with your clothes. Wear them and make a test recording with your webcam. Clothes that fit well when you stand may do strange and unusual things when you're sitting.

Jewelry and Accessories

Earrings should be no larger than a quarter, not dangle or swing, and be non-reflective. Most necklaces tend to be gorgeous in person, but if we start looking at it while you're talking, we may miss the essence of your brief comments. If you wear neck jewelry, make sure it has a non-reflective finish.

Solution for a Man's Bald Spot

In webcam interviews, there will usually be an overhead light that glares on a man's oily bald spot(s). Before the interview, wipe those areas with rubbing alcohol. It will eliminate the glare.

In Early TV, Blue Was White

In the early days of television news, men were told to wear light blue shirts. That's because they were shooting black-and-white film. A white shirt glowed in the harsh light and high-contrast film. A blue shirt looked white.

With today's color cameras, white looks white, and blue looks blue.

But the automatic sensor in today's cameras reads the general light level coming through the lens. Light clothing makes the aperture of the camera lens constrict, just as the iris in the human eye does. Dark clothing does the opposite (more on this in the *Lighting and Background* chapter)

Generally, your clothes for television should be subdued. Plain, solid colors are best. Stay away from stripes, checks and bold prints. The electronics in modern video cameras can make patterns seem to ripple and pulsate. Make the clothes fit the story.

My simple rule: If we remember what you were wearing, you wore the wrong thing.

Don't Get a Haircut

If you know a webcam interview is imminent, don't go to the beauty salon or the barber shop. We will probably be able to tell that you spruced up for the interview.

Remember, this is supposedly a spontaneous, unrehearsed conversation, not a formal portrait or glamour shoot.

I was fairly new to television when I covered the 1972 Republican National Convention in Miami Beach. There was a demonstration where the crowd became violent and police used teargas.

Effects of Teargas

I do not do teargas well. I get wheezy and my eyes get terribly irritated. I've been temporarily blinded by teargas.

On that night in 1972, I ran to the apartment WPLG had rented as a studio, across from the Convention Center. I told them what was happening in the street. In addition to my bleary eyes, I was drenched with sweat.

"Get in the chair," a producer told me. "We'll do a live cut-in."

"Let me wash my face and comb my hair," I said.

"No, no, no," the producer said. "You look like shit. That will tell us more than anything you're gonna say."

Wear Your Eyeglasses

If you normally wear eyeglasses, wear them for the interview. Without them, your eyes will have to work harder. You'll squint. There will be a crease through a man's sideburns and depressions in your nose where the glasses were before the interview.

But Not Sunglasses

But don't wear dark glasses for webcam interviews. In this culture, you're supposed to look people in the eye when you talk to them. The stereotyped movie hoodlum wears dark glasses during conversations - perhaps to hide the evil thoughts his eyes would reveal if we could see them.

Beware - glasses that darken in sunlight might also turn dark if you've set up auxiliary lighting for your webcam.

If you're going to do a lot of television interviews, have your optician treat your eyeglass lenses with the invisible, anti-reflective coating that television reporters and anchors use. It's very much like the coating on a camera lens.

Reading the Details

Normally, I advise clients to NEVER read speeches or statements. Unless you've worked in broadcasting, you don't read well. It seems canned and insincere. But there is an exception.

As a television reporter, I developed a technique for live remotes that let me read exact words from an important document. It added authority and credibility. If three legislators had been indicted for bribery, I'd do the live shot in front of the courthouse, with the indictment in my hand.

"Let Me Read It to You"

Off-the-cuff, I'd summarize what had happened, then say, "Let me read to you what the grand jury found." I'd have a paragraph high-lighted. I'd read it, then continue in my own words until I reached another section where I wanted to use exactly what the grand jury reported.

You can use the same technique in a webcam interview.

Animation and Body English

You will be much more effective in a webcam interview if you talk the same way you do in normal conversation. I'd like the people watching the interview to say to themselves: Did he/she know this was being recorded?

In normal conversations, people gesture with their hands. They have facial animation. A raised eyebrow. A frown. They shake their heads to emphasize something they disapprove of. They lean forward to emphasize a comment. It becomes a physical exclamation point.

And we pause. To let the idea sink in. The half-second pause is a WONDERFUL ingredient for webcam interviews. It gives the listener time to digest what you've just said. It also provides an easy editing point.

Creating Sound Bites

I estimate that about 35,000 people are interviewed by the news media in America every day. This is hard to believe, but I already know exactly what the reporters are going to ask in about 90 per cent of those interviews.

It doesn't matter where the interview takes place. Doesn't matter who the reporter is - who is being interviewed - doesn't even matter what the story is about. I know the key question:

How Do You Feel . . .?

In virtually every news interview, the reporter will ask how you feel about something.

The perennial question has been institutionalized by a TV news story formula - the Sony Sandwich. It has spread to all news media.

Disguising the Question

Reporters are so aware of their trite question, they try to disguise it. But it is still the search for the human perspective.

- Tell me - what you were thinking, just before the plane hit the water?

- When the officer walked in with your baby in his arms, what was it like?

- What was your reaction when you become aware you had been bilked by your financial advisor?

- Did you think you were going to die?

Someday, we may go through that same experience. We want to know how it feels to do what you did ... see what you saw ... hear what you heard.

What Was It Like to Be There?

How do you feel is usually asking, "What was it like to be there?" That has always been the essence of storytelling. If a ghost story is told skillfully, I shudder and look over my shoulder in the dark.

Tell me the story of a blind child who can see for the first time, and I get a lump in my throat.

When she tells me what she's feeling, I may cry.

The Human Perspective

Interviews inject the human perspective in news stories. Few people outside the news media understand this basic purpose for the "feeling" question that will elicit the quote or the sound bite the storyteller is looking for.

It is sandwiched between the facts the reporter gives at the beginning, and the conclusion drawn at the end.

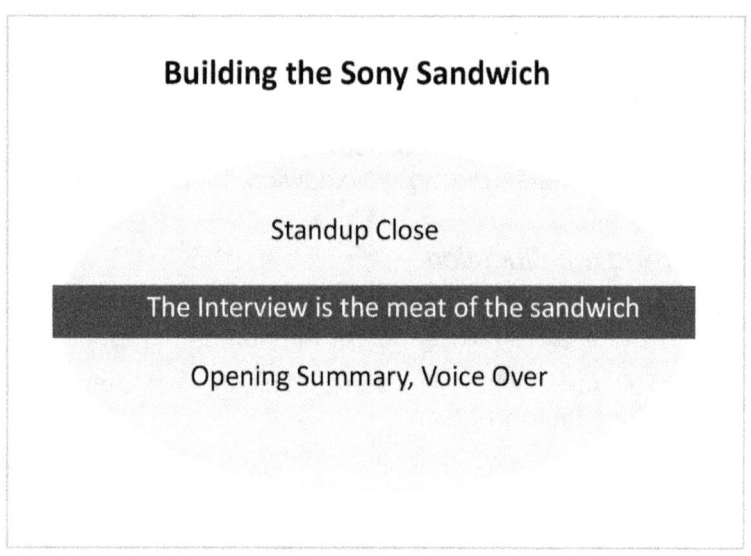

Building the Sony Sandwich

Standup Close

The Interview is the meat of the sandwich

Opening Summary, Voice Over

The Sony Sandwich Formula

Something you say during your webcam interview with a TV reporter will become the meat in a Sony Sandwich - the "sound bite."

It gives the story warmth and personality, emotion and flavor, color and dimension.

If it's a network story, they rarely use more than 10 seconds from an interview. A local station may let you speak a few seconds longer. This story formula is sometimes called a "package."

The beginning of the Sony Sandwich is the bottom half of the bun. The reporter quickly sketches the scenario. It is a summary of the story. Sometimes only a sentence or two.

We frequently have not seen the reporter yet.

The Voice-Over Summary

The summary is delivered V/O (voice/over) while we are shown video of the place or event the story is about. After the reporter has set up the basic facts, we go to a central figure in the story.

The Key Question

That person is asked something like:

- How did you feel when you learned your son was alive?

- (On election night) How does it feel to lose after 24 years in the Senate?

- How does it feel to win the lottery?

- How do you feel about the President's proposal?

- How do you feel, now that your company has gone bankrupt?

- Do you feel this proposal is necessary?

Topping off the Sandwich

And then the reporter closes out the story. Often with a standup, looking into the camera, in front of the spot the story is about. The reporter summarizes, telling us what to expect next. Here's the formula closing:

What Does it All Mean?

What does it all mean? Only time will tell. I'm Tom Trite, Channel Four, Action News.

People in certain professions are interviewed more often than others. The ones who get the hang of it find reporters coming back to them on future stories. They make the reporter's job so much easier. Unfortunately, some careers tend to create poor prospects for interviews.

Career Influence On Camera Style

Doctors, lawyers, scientists and accountants are often terrible on camera. They speak their own, professional jargon, as though we, too, had Ph.Ds in their specialty. They provide dry, lengthy, logical, step-by-step reasoning, with lots of footnotes. The subject matter is complicated. The simplest question takes three minutes to answer.

This kind of interview is a horror to edit. The people interviewed call the next day to complain that they were quoted out of context. On camera, they often sound like robotic voice synthesizers. They've been conditioned to talk that way by writing too many reports, reading too many articles written by colleagues, and by testifying in court.

Human Synthesizers

The cop who just caught two armed robbers after a shootout speaks very normally until the camera comes. Then he says:

> My unit was dispatched to 4481 Ocean Street at nineteen hundred hours. As I approached, Code Three, I observed two white males rapidly exiting the dispatched location in an easterly direction with weapons drawn. When the perpetrators observed my vehicle, they commenced firing. One projectile impacted my vehicle. I then returned fire.

What Did He Say?

What did he say? I think he said:

"As I rolled up, these two guys with guns were running out of the jewelry store. They saw the patrol car and started shooting. When the first bullet hit my windshield, I jumped out and shot back." Which leads to the reporter's question:

"You ever been shot at before?"

"Nope."

"How did it feel?"

"Scared the hell out of me."

You can probably guess which section of the interview is certain to be included in the Sony Sandwich.

What Are We Afraid Of?

Survey after survey has shown that stage fright is America's biggest fear. Bigger than war, cancer, divorce, dying in a plane or car crash. What are we so afraid of onstage?

I think we're afraid of looking stupid.

People in front of a camera often talk non-conversation because they're afraid they'll make a mistake and look dumb.

What Will the Boss Think?

They're not sure the boss will like the idea of their talking to a TV reporter.

So they cram and memorize, to avoid mistakes. They want to be walking, infallible encyclopedias. But they're boring, and we don't even listen.

Becoming What You Most Fear

Applicants being interviewed by webcam for a job often do the same thing. They can look like stupid drones. Robots with a recorded message. The one thing they most fear.

Other people deal with on-camera stress by drawing themselves into tight little knots, making their voices small and flat, as they say every word very carefully.

They pause a lot. On TV, they are deadly. More than five seconds, and everybody in the audience will be snoring.

The Original Story Formula

The Sony Sandwich evolved from the original American news story formula - developed by newspapers in the 1800s - the Inverted Pyramid.

At the beginning of the story - into the first paragraph, if possible - the reporter tried to cram all the important facts. Who, What, When, Where, Why.

From that broad beginning, the story narrowed down to a point at the bottom where unimportant details were thrown in. Pure trivia.

The inverted pyramid had several practical purposes. Correspondents in faraway places (St. Louis was the edge of civilization in those days) sent their stories to New York or Washington by telegraph.

The Telegraph was Unreliable

The telegraph was not very reliable. So if it failed sometime during transmission, the home office would at least have the important stuff. If the entire story reached the newspaper, readers knew they could drop off in mid-story and not miss anything critical.

In those days, newspaper stories were set in lead type. Down in the composing room, they had to fit each line of type into a page form before the newspaper went to press. If the type didn't fit, the employees in the composing room were told to cut from the bottom until it did fit.

Throwing Away Paragraphs

Just throw away the last paragraph, they were told. Maybe the last two paragraphs. There were barrels where the lead type was thrown to be recycled. The typesetters were not editors. They were craftsmen. As a result, stories sometimes seemed to have been edited with a chain saw.

The Sandwich Spreads

Because the Sony Sandwich works so well, both radio and newspapers adopted it for their own use. Understanding the formula will help you craft a quote that will be used exactly as you said it - without editing - in newspapers, radio, TV, or Internet podcasts.

Avoiding Misquotes

If you can learn to do this, you'll seldom be misquoted or taken out of context. You'll find your interviews go very quickly. As soon as reporters hear the magic, formula quote, they tell you goodbye.

And they'll ask you for more webcam interviews in the future for stories in your area of expertise.

The FACE Formula

I invented the FACE Formula to help you remember what kind of quote the reporter is looking for. If you're the subject of the interview, and we're going to see your face on TV. Keep these factors in mind:

F eelings

A nalysis

C ompelling C's

E nergy

Let's look at each factor in the formula:

Feelings

Let the audience know what you're feeling. Go back from time to time and review the Sony Sandwich formula to help you reflexively craft quotes that begin with how you feel.

That first phrase sets us up to receive your reasons for feeling that way. Like:

"I'm really angry about this." Or sad, happy, encouraged, disappointed, afraid, surprised, confident ... You get the idea.

Analysis

Give them your assessment of the situation. In one phrase or sentence, tell them what the bottom line is. The audience wants your expert opinion on the subject. That's why the reporter is talking to you.

But to avoid the cutting room floor, the expert must be able to translate into everyday language. Analysis interviews often deal with statistics.

Numbers Must Have Perspective

If you use numbers, they are meaningless unless you put the numbers in perspective.

Many experts speak in strange tongues. After the reporter has said that experts claim there is no danger from the accident within the nuclear power plant, we see an interview with an internationally recognized scientist. He says on camera:

We've put the effluent through exhaustive electron microscopy plus radiofluorocarbon laser analysis and we come up with a count of point four, seven, zero micro-mini roentgens.

What did he say?

Translated, I think he said: You'd get more radiation sitting in front of a TV for two hours than you would if you took a bath in the water that leaked out.

The Compelling C's

Most news stories revolve around at least one of these basic elements. Notice the feeling words:

Catastrophe - "I'm afraid we're facing a global disaster if we don't change the way we dispose of toxic waste."

Crisis - "I'm astounded by their stupidity. The tidal surge will sweep across the highway and cut off their escape route if they don't leave now."

Conflict - "I hate him and everything he stands for. I'll fight him to my last breath."

Change - "I'm confident things are going to be different around here after the election, when we win control of the Legislature."

Crime and Corruption - "I grieve for the victims of this horrible crime. And I won't rest until they catch who did it."

Color - (They used to call it human interest.) "I'm really amused. Anyone who believes that also believes thunder curdles milk."

Celebrities - "I'm awed by his technical skill. He can manipulate that computer the way Michael Jordan controls a basketball."

Energy

There is one major difference in talking on camera and talking to your friends in their living room. To be effective on camera, your conversation needs to project energy. On-screen, you will ALWAYS be more boring than you are in real life.

Like a salesperson who must believe in the product, you must show that you truly believe what you're saying.

Since so many stories for television news involve conflict and imminent danger, you must convince us - through the energy you invest in what you're saying - that we ought to be concerned, too.

Executive Cool = Dull

Some executives in high-pressure jobs adopt a cool, clinical personality that says to their employees, "I know exactly what I'm doing. If the building were on fire, I would lead you to safety." That deliberate, slow, calculating style can appear, - on TV - to be boredom, disinterest, or a mask for insecurity.

You Need to See and Hear Yourself

I constantly tell my clients that they need to see themselves on camera to know what they really look like. In our minds, we have imbedded high school yearbook photos of ourselves. That image distorts our perception of ourselves.

The mirror lies. The person I see when I shave is about 20 years younger, 20 pounds lighter than the person on my webcam screen.

A webcam is an ideal learning tool. You can record practice interviews and replay them instantly until you're happy with the results.

The Boring Phenomenon

Be aware that there is a major distortion when we watch interviews on television or a computer monitor. Time slows down. You may not catch this as you watch your own performance. But others will.

Unless you inject energy into what you say, our perception of the person on screen is that you are incredibly dull and boring.

The Slow Motion Experience

Why does that happen? I think I have the answer. Have you ever been in a life-threatening crisis where everything seemed to go into slow motion?

I've questioned thousands of people in my workshops about these experiences. It seems to be universal.

In the moments before the car crash, they watched the on-coming car spinning gracefully, edging closer, as they carefully analyzed whether it would hit them.

Life-Threatening Crises

A pilot told about losing an engine on takeoff. It seemed to take half a day to turn the plane and get it back on the ground.

A scuba diver in a cave ran out of air and made a desperate attempt to reach the surface. He lost consciousness, and would have drowned. But he was rescued by his buddies and resuscitated. He said the time he was struggling to reach the surface before he blacked out was only a few seconds. But it seemed more like hours.

A woman thrown up through her car's sunroof when it rolled over said she felt like she was hovering in mid-air, watching her car turning slowly below her.

Shooting As He Fell

A cop was shot at close range. The bullet knocked him on his back. As he fell, he was able to pull his pistol and fire three times before he hit the ground.

It was easy to do, he said, because it seemed like he was suspended in mid-air for about five minutes. He said he even had time to aim the shot that hit his assailant in the chest.

The technical name for the phenomenon is tachypsychia. Part of it is caused by the sudden dump of adrenaline into your bloodstream. The other factor is your total focus on what is happening.

Our Perception Changes Time

It is my theory that when we watch an interview on a computer monitor or television screen, we are focused just enough to change our perception of time.

I see this happen regularly in my seminars. I videotape an interview and then we have instant replay.

The person who seemed to be speaking in a normal voice just a few seconds ago now seems to have lost energy and conviction.

I know the replay is accurate. It is our perception as we focus that robs the interview of its energy and passion.

By practicing with recorded webcam interviews, you can study yourself. You can learn to inject just the right amount of energy to make our perception of you on the screen match what we would see in real life.

Don't Overdo It

Just don't overdo it, so you seem shrill or obsessed. There is a different line for everyone. And a gender gap between how we perceive men and women. Only practice will find that line.

Forget About Memorizing

In preparing for a webcam interview, don't memorize or write out a script. It makes the interview seem staged and rehearsed.

I recommend that before the interview, you go over in your mind the main points you'd like to include. You need to have that central theme in your head, and some sub-sections that connect to that central idea. No more than three.

If you're afraid the stress of the interview will make you forget, write yourself a cheat sheet, the same way students cheat on exams.

Using a Cheat Sheet

The cheat sheet should be one-word cues - bullet points - that will refresh your memory if your mind goes blank. Put the cheat sheet where you can glance down and see it But ONLY IF YOU NEED TO.

The trick is to look thoughtful, pause and glance down as if you're thinking deeply, then look back at the webcam to finish the thought.

This is a natural head movement in normal conversation. Be careful about setting up a rhythm of repeatedly looking down and then back at the webcam. If you do that, we'll know you're reading.

Nobody will know you cheated if you do it right.

A Psychological Crutch

Just writing the key points will help you remember. Having the cheat sheet handy is an assuring psychological crutch. If it's there, you probably won't need it.

Remember – you have to condense, condense, condense. In public speaking courses, the instructor gives you a subject and forces you to make an immediate, extemporaneous talk. The exercise teaches you to think and talk on your feet.

Some Training Exercises

To train yourself for webcam interviews, try to say how you feel about a difficult topic – and three reasons why you feel that way – in 12 seconds or less.

Pick tough, complicated subjects and practice with your webcam. In one sentence, say how you feel – and why – about difficult subjects like:

- Legalized abortion
- Gun control
- Capital punishment
- Prayer in schools
- Ethnic job quotas
- Illegal immigration
- Taxes and government spending

There is no quick miracle drug, no magic diet, no futuristic exercise machine to make you an instant success. It takes tough, conscientious mental calisthenics if you want to be truly good at it.

This exercise, practiced regularly, will develop your mental agility for condensing what you know and feel about complicated subjects.

Congressional Pros

The real pros are congressional leaders who've been interviewed several times a day for 20 years. They develop stopwatches in their heads. Before the camera rolls, they discuss the story with the reporter. They get some idea of how their quotes will be used.

The Quickie Interview

"How much time do you need?" the senator asks, clearing his throat and brushing his hair aside.

"About 12 seconds," the reporter tells him.

"OK. Ready?"

"Rolling."

The senator speaks for 12 seconds. Perhaps 11. Sometimes, 13. And then he stops. He has learned the language, and the game. He edits himself. There can be no distortion. He is rarely quoted out of context. The entire process has taken less than five minutes.

You Can Do It, Too

Most of those who've learned to speak in sound bites did it the hard way, through trial and error. For many, it became a self-defense tactic. The news media are kinder to some people than others.

One person's slip is never aired. Another, similar stumble becomes the comedy element in tonight's news.

Learn From Others' Mistakes

Watch and listen to interviews on TV newcasts. Make notes on the people who are effective. Learn from the mistakes and blunders of other people.

If you can learn how to speak media language, and give a formula response to the formula question, you almost guarantee they'll use what you said, exactly as you said it.

With no editing, misquoting or taking out of context.

You're the Expert

Often, the person being interviewed is an authority, whose assessment of the situation is important to our understanding it. In court testimony, witnesses are not allowed to express their opinions or feelings. Unless they are certified as expert witnesses. Only then they can tell the jury how they feel about the evidence.

When you become the subject of a media interview, it's often because you're the expert witness who can put things in perspective. When reporters ask experts how they feel, they're really asking for opinion or analysis.

Verbal Shorthand

Words that express feeling tell us a lot very quickly. They are verbal shorthand - headline words that communicate like no others in our language. They get to the heart of the story, and set us up to hear your reasons for feeling that way.

When the reporter asks how you feel about something, it can mean, "What do you think about this? - What is your reaction to the situation? - What is your opinion?" But we will understand your reaction - your opinion - your conclusion - much more clearly if you tell us how you FEEL.

News stories are so formularized, it is almost a paint-by-numbers process. I've collected a list of words, from which at least one will fit virtually any news interview in which you're asked that key question. Take your pick.

Words That Say How You Feel

A Abandoned, Abused, Afraid, Aggravated, Alienated, Alone, Amazed, Ambushed, Amused, Angry, Anxious, Ashamed, Astonished, Astounded

B Besieged, Betrayed, Blessed, Bored, Bothered, Burned out, Battered, Bedazzled, Broken, Blinded

C Caught in the middle, Certain, Challenged, Chagrined, Cheated, Concerned, Confident, Conflicted, Confused, Conned, Cozy, Crazy

D Dazzled, Deceived, Delighted, Deserted, Disappointed, Dismayed, Disorganized, Distraught, Distressed, Doubtful

E Ecstatic, Elated Embarrassed, Encouraged, Energized, Enthusiastic, Envious, Excited, Exhausted, Exposed

F Fearful, Fed up, Forgiven, Forgiving, Frantic, Free, Friendly, Frightened, Frustrated, Fenced in

G Glad, Glorious, Grateful, Gratified, Great! Grief-stricken, Guilty, Gullible, Gutted

H Happy, Harried, Hate (I hate it!), Haunted, Helpless, High, Hobbled, Hollow, Homicidal, Honored, Hoodwinked, Hopeful, Hopeless, Horrendous, Horrible, Horrified, Hounded, Humble, Humiliated, Hungry, Hurt

I Impatient, Impotent, Ineffective, Insecure, Inspired, Insulted, Intrigued, Invaded, Irritated, Isolated

J Jaded, Jealous, Jilted, Jinxed, Jolted, Joyful, Jubilant, Justified

L Livid, Lonely, Love (I love it!), Loser (Like a loser), Lucky, Lively

M Mad, Maligned, Marvelous, Misguided, Misunderstood, Mortified, Mystified

N Naked, Nauseated, Neglected, Negligent, Nostalgic, Nurtured

O Offended, On top of the world, Optimistic, Out of touch, Outgunned, Outnumbered, Outraged, Overjoyed, Overwhelmed

P Paranoid, Parental, Peeved, Pessimistic, Pissed, Pleased, Powerful, Powerless, Proud, Put down, Put out, Puzzled

R Ready, Recharged Regretful, Reinforced, Rejoice, Rejuvenated, Relieved, Reminiscent, Resentful, Responsive, Rested

S Sad, Safe, Sated, Satisfied, Saturated, Scared, Secure, Shocked, Shunned, Sick, Skeptical, Sorry, Stupid, Supportive, Sure, Surprised, Surrounded, Swindled, Sympathetic, Shaken

T Targeted, Terrible, Terrific, Terrified, Tired, Torn, Trampled, Traumatized

U Uncertain, Undaunted, Under control, Underwhelmed, Undone, Unforgiving, Unjustly accused, Unsatisfied, Unwanted, Unworthy, Used

V Victimized, Victorious, Vulnerable

W Warm, Weak, Weary, Weepy, Winner (Like a winner), Wonderful, Worried, Worn out, Wounded

Condition Words

Some of the feeling words in the list above are not real feelings. They are conditions that convey several emotions or strong feelings.

When you say, "I feel betrayed," you tell us - with just one word - that you feel angry, deceived, abandoned, vulnerable. If you feel surrounded, you are feeling insecure, outnumbered, overwhelmed.

Interviews add flavor and spice to a story. Once the conflict, the catastrophe, the crisis is established, we want to hear the participants. We want to know how they feel about it. Their reaction to it.

Guaranteed- Sound Bites

Sound bites they'll use for sure:

- "I'm embarrassed. The mayor has made a terrible mistake."

- "It's frightening. This guy is completely bonkers. He'll take us back to the Stone Age."

- "I wasn't afraid - I was just terribly sad, that I'd never see my son again."

- "Fantastic. After the surgery, I feel like a kid again."

A Word of Caution:

There are a few rare times when showing too much emotion on camera can be hazardous to your career. We don't expect a homicide detective to break down at a murder scene. Unless the victim is his partner, or his own child.

Some history: Edmund Muskie may have lost his campaign for the Democratic presidential nomination in 1972 when he became teary during a speech in the snow in New Hampshire. He was defending his wife after a newspaper editorial defamed her. In those days, Americans thought that made him appear weak.

The Rules Began to Change

But then society's expectations began to change. During the televised 1988 presidential debates, Democratic nominee Gov. Michael Dukakis - an opponent of capital punishment - was asked how he would feel on that issue if his wife was a rape or murder victim.

Dukakis showed no emotion. His answer was academic, distant, unfeeling. People in the audience thought: What sort of man is this, who doesn't react to his wife being violated or killed? His nickname became "Zorba the accountant." He did not win.

A Kinder, Gentler President

In that same campaign, George H. W. Bush's media experts asked focus groups what kind of President they wanted. Based on that research, Bush promised to be a "kinder, gentler President."

In television interviews, Bush began to talk about his family as sensitive, caring people. The Bushes, he said, show what they feel, and sometimes the men are not afraid to cry.

Schwarzkopf's Tears

One of the most dramatic demonstrations of how the rules were changing came three years later. Barbara Walters interviewed Army Gen. Norman Schwarzkopf in Saudi Arabia for _20/20_. It was 1991, shortly after the Persian Gulf War ended. Schwarzkopf had been the commanding general in that war.

"Stormin' Norman" talked about how much he missed his family, half a world away, and the tears welled in his eyes. When Walters asked about his dead father, who had also been a general, the tears came again. "I'm sure he'd be proud of me," Schwarzkopf said, his lower lip trembling.

Generals Don't Cry

There was a long pause in the interview.

"You know," Walters said, "The old picture of generals - is that generals don't cry."

"Sure they do," Schwarzkopf shot back, naming Civil War generals Ulysses Grant and William Tecumseh Sherman. "And these were the tough old guys. Lee cried at the loss of human life, the pressures that were brought to bear. Lincoln cried.

"Frankly, any man that doesn't cry scares me a little bit. I don't think I would like a man who was incapable of enough emotion to get tears in his eyes every now and then. That's not a human being."

September 11, 2001

A sea change of attitude about showing emotion in America came 10 years later, after the terrorist attacks of Sept. 11, 2001. Police officers, firefighters, and reporters wept openly on television as the news media covered the carnage and its aftermath.

And so did those watching the story unfold. Americans became more human, more able to express their caring and their grief.

Howard Dean's Scream

As I said earlier, you need to see yourself on camera to know where the emotional line is for you. Remember Howard Dean's candidacy to be the Democratic nominee for President in 2004?

He became so overly enthusiastic at a rally after the Iowa caucuses, some voters felt he really didn't have the demeanor to be President.

Obama's Failure to Show Emotion

As President Barack Obama struggled with the economic recession, health care and two wars after he took office in 2009, his public approval ratings began to plummet. His cold, intellectual way of dealing with major issues made people feel he was distant and uncaring.

Not until the incumbent Democrats in Congress were trounced in the November, 2010 elections did Obama go back to the enthusiastic style he had displayed when he was running for election.

Mitt Romney's Lukewarm Support

In the 2012 presidential campaign, analysts struggled to figure out why Republicans were lukewarm about Mitt Romney. The best guess was that his life of privilege and wealth had conditioned him to not care about those with less wealth, and to be protective about his private life and his inner feelings.

That gave many in the middle class a concern that he was not one of them. That he did not react to life as they did. That he would not make critical decisions the way they would.

Sandy Hook Murders

And then another watershed event occurred. Twenty-six teachers and first-graders were killed in a mass murder at Sandy Hook Elementary School in December, 2012. Barrack Obama, many reporters, anchor people and police officers wept on camera as they talked about the shootings.

And viewers, choked up in their living rooms, felt it was perfectly OK for the journalists and first responders to show their feelings, too.

Gender Conflicts

There are also gender conflicts in the culture. In their childhood, men who are now middle-aged or older were taught not to show their feelings. Men don't cry, they were told. Men don't show fear, or pain.

Women are caught in a crossfire as the culture shifts. Cry at the office and the men in power are likely to invoke the old standards that said showing emotion was a sign of weakness.

"Just like a woman," they mutter under their breath.

America still has many double standards for men and women. An angry, determined man is called aggressive. Bold.

An angry woman may be called shrill. Bitchy. Emotionally unstable. Hormonally challenged.

That's why seeing yourself on video is so important. Everybody has a different threshold in expressing how you feel without appearing to go overboard.

Show Your Humanity

I'm not suggesting that you cry in every interview. My goal for you is to show your humanity. If you do, those quotes will be used, and used exactly as you spoke them. In context. No misquotes.

The formula that reporters use is so predictable, I make a bet with my seminar groups: Send me a transcript of your next media interview. Print, radio, television. Doesn't matter. I'll buy you dinner if I can't pick the quote or sound bite the reporter used when the story was printed or broadcast.

It will always be the quote that tells us how you feel. I've made the bet with more than 100,000 people, and I've never lost.

Think of Your Audience

Listening to one end of a telephone conversation, you can usually tell who's on the other end. If it's long distance, most people tend to talk louder. Subconsciously, they think they have to speak up to be heard clearly a thousand miles away.

We slow down if we sense that the person at the other end of the line is old, or has a foreign accent. We change the tone of our voice if we're talking to a child, or a lover. The same kind of subtle changes take place when people talk in front of cameras and microphones.

An Audience of One or Two

If they know they're being recorded, many people reflexively talk as if they're making a speech in a huge auditorium. There may be half a million people - perhaps more - out there listening. With a crowd that large, you subconsciously think you must make sure the people in the back row hear what you have to say.

But they're not all in one, humongous auditorium.

The video audience is one or two people. It is Joe Sixpack and Aunt Millie, sitting in the living room or kitchen, six or eight feet from the TV set. It is one person, watching a podcast on a computer monitor 18 inches away.

One of the secrets of video interviews is to keep that tiny audience of one or two people in mind.

Think of Someone Else

If the person on your webcam screen is a famous TV personality, it may help you to imagine you're talking to someone else. Someone you know well. Your spouse, a neighbor, the cashier at the restaurant where you have lunch.

In your mind, you're talking to one of them, not the reporter or anchorperson.

Mind-Set & Body Language

Changing your mind-set will change your body language. In the noise and confusion of a political rally, a candidate holds up his arms and flashes a big grin to communicate warmth and charm as he tries to woo the crowd.

He uses a very different kind of smile and body language later that night if he's trying to seduce a beautiful woman sitting across the table from him in a quiet restaurant.

You Don't Need to Project

If you think of a large audience, you will instinctively project your voice to reach them. You don't need to do that.

But it takes a lot of practice to squelch that natural inclination. Today's microphones are so sensitive they can pick up a whisper across a room.

For video interviews, the most powerful message is delivered with a whispered shout. It is emotional emphasis and intensity - not loudness - that will get your point across most effectively.

Clinton's Town Meetings

Former President Bill Clinton's best style for TV was always town meetings. He was at his best talking to a specific person, not the entire crowd. He still is.

Focusing On Just One Person

He takes a step or two toward the person who asks a question. He maintains intense eye contact to enhance our perception that he is totally absorbed in this very personal conversation with someone whose opinion matters. We like that about famous people.

Remember, the webcam is not one of your professional colleagues. It's somebody you just met at a dinner party, who knows absolutely nothing about your job and won't understand its jargon.

The Camera Spots Phonies

The camera detects phonies. Bring to the conversation the real person inside you, not a front. Let your emotions show, if they're real. You can be angry, or sad, pleased with yourself or your organization, shocked or dismayed at what you've just learned.

The reporter will not use many facts or figures when your sound bite is chosen to include in the story. Nor your recitation of the facts. There is not enough time. You probably don't have the skill to boil down the facts extemporaneously.

Writing Shot Takes a Long Time

Even experienced reporters have trouble doing that.

To condense them to 10 or 15 seconds can require a half-hour at the keyboard, eliminating a word, rewriting a phrase to save another few seconds.

A famous quote, attributed to several people: "I'm writing you a long letter because I didn't have time to write a short one."

Tell Me a Story

Another important way to persuade the reporter that you know what you're talking about - or to reinforce your position - is to make a statement and then tell a story that illustrates that statement. Transitions like:

We MUST do something about the way we care for wounded veterans. I was at the local veterans' hospital yesterday and talked with a man who ...

Draw Us a Picture

Set up your story by drawing us a picture. A quick phrase like "I could tell he had once been an athlete. Very muscular, except for the withered leg that no longer works."

Television news is always pressed to save time. But a well-told story can stretch those limits as part of a sound bite.

The Story is Convincing

Saying how you feel, and then telling your story reinforces your opinion and helps to get your point across.

You should have a library of transition phrases that smoothly take you to your story. Like:

- For instance ...

- Let me give you an example ...

- I wish you could have seen ...

- I came to that conclusion after I ...

- I didn't feel this way until I ...

Your Listening Face

During a webcam interview, we will also see you listening. Be aware of your facial expression while you're listening to the person on the other side of the conversation.

Your listening face needs to tell us that you're comfortable, self-confident, alert, glad to be here.

Without saying a word, you can also make a very strong statement by telegraphing that you agree - or vehemently disagree - with the person who is speaking at the other end of the connection.

Where Did That Idea Come From?

A frown or "what the hell" expression telegraphs that you think the person speaking is absolutely wrong. Or crazy.

A slight smile and nod puts your stamp of approval on what-ever is being said at the other end of the conversation.

A laugh says your opponent's idea is truly crazy.

During Presidential debates, well-trained candidates have learned how to contradict and criticize their opponents without saying a word. In that format, the screen is often split so we can see both candidates.

As an opponent talks about a program or a position, we see the other candidate's face express disgust, dislike or astonishment with a smile, a nod, a frown, an eye roll.

The silent listening face can be more eloquent than the spoken words.

Build a Backdrop Frame

The best way I've found to create a plain backdrop is to make a five-foot-square frame out of PVC pipe and hang fabric on it.

It's easy to assemble and take apart. The pieces can easily be stored.

The pipe and fittings are available at home improvement and hardware stores. It's inexpensive, lightweight and easy to cut.

The fabric can be a lightweight blanket of any shade or color. A twin-size blanket will give you enough coverage for a frame that's five feet square.

See more about the importance of the background in the *Lighting and Background* chapter.

Materials & Tools You'll Need

All PVC pipe and fittings for this frame are ¾ inch, Schedule 40. The pipe comes in 10-foot lengths. You can buy pipe by the foot, but it's often cheaper to buy entire lengths and cut it yourself.

I recommend a scissor-type cutting tool rather than a saw.

A hammer will help with assembly and disassembly.

You'll also need a ⅛ - inch drill bit, a screw driver, and about a dozen #8 screws. At the store, they'll usually cut the 10-foot pipe in half for free, so it will fit in your car. Or you can take your cutting tool with you and do it yourself.

PVC Pipe & Fittings (about $10)

3 pieces of pipe 60 inches long (five feet)

1 piece of pipe 54 inches long

2 pieces of pipe 2 inches long

4 pieces of pipe 24 inches long

4 90° elbows

4 tees

2 four-way connectors

Four-Way Connectors

All stores don't stock the four-way connectors. (above) If you don't find them, you can use 4 tees instead to make the cross-legs that keep the frame upright.

If you use the 4-tee substitute (above), the 54-inch pipe in the materials list will be 48 inches, and you'll need four 2-inch pieces of pipe instead of two. The additional two-inchers connect the tees, as shown here (before the tees are tapped together).

How to Assemble the Frame

Start by using the four elbows to connect all three one-piece sides together, into a square, with one side missing. Put it on a level surface (the floor, or your driveway) stand on the pipe, and drive the elbows onto the pipes. It should lie flat.

If it's not quite square, stand on a corner or tap it with the hammer to bring it into line. The pipe and fittings are very tough. You can't hurt them.

Notice how the shorter, bottom pipe is connected to the other sides of the frame. A two-inch piece of pipe connects the four-way connector to each elbow.

With the four-sided assembly still lying flat, tap a 24-inch pipe into each of the four-way connectors.

Now It Will Stay Upright

Now you can raise the assembly and it will stay upright while you tap the remaining 24-inch pipes into the opposite sides of the four-ways.

Tees go on each end of the 24-inch pipes and are secured with screws. Their function is to help you disassemble the frame. PVC pipe, once it's tapped into a fitting, can be difficult to remove. But it will come apart easily with a tap of your hammer on one of those tees. It also disconnects if you twist it with a pipe wrench.

The 24-inch pipes become the base to keep the frame stable. You might be able to shorten them and maintain stability, if you don't have enough room where you're using the frame.

Portions of the frame you don't want to disassemble when you tap a fitting should be held in place with #8 screws, ¾-inch long. Drill a ⅛-inch hole through both the fitting and the pipe to take the screws.

Don't Glue the Parts Together

Don't be tempted to use PVC glue. Glued fittings won't hold if you tap them very much in assembly and disassembly.

One spot that will definitely need screws is the elbow at each end of the bottom pipe. This is where the frame will have the most stress to stay upright with fabric attached.

Bundling the Parts for Storage

When disassembled, you can bundle the pipes together for storage. If the five-foot length won't fit your storage space, cut each of the long pipes in half and use a connector fitting to bring the bundle down to 30 inches long.

Any fabric can be draped over the top of the frame and held in place with clothespins, safety pins, or large binder clips available at office supply stores.

Weight at the Bottom of Your Fabric

You may also want to use weighted binder clips attached to the bottom of the fabric to make any wrinkles less noticeable. If you have enough fabric left at the bottom, you can also hold it down and keep it taut with books and other stuff.

A lightweight blanket works fine. I sometimes use a piece of heavier, terrycloth black fabric when I want the backdrop to be less visible.

Distance Between Backdrop & Webcam

Place the backdrop as far away from the webcam as possible, still keeping the edges of the frame out of your webcam shot.

The distance helps with shadows, and will perhaps put the backdrop out of focus (see more on focus and depth of field in the _Lighting and Background_ chapter).

It would be ideal to have you in sharp focus and the background fuzzy. But the automatic exposure in most webcams doesn't give you a lot of control over that.

About the Author

Clarence Jones is an on-camera coach. He learned a lot about interviewing as a newspaper reporter, and then became one of the most-honored reporters in American television.

After reporting for 30 years, he wrote a book on the subject - *Winning with the News Media - A Self Defense Manual When You're the News.* The book immediately took off, and he reporting career to launch a consulting firm that specializes in on-camera training of executives in government and corporate America.

His day job is CEO of that company. He runs his media consulting firm out of a home office in Bradenton, on the west coast of Florida. He has published six non-fiction books (listed below) and is now writing a novel (his first) in which a TV investigative reporter tries to solve a kidnap-murder case in Miami.

They say you should write about topics you know really well.

Clarence is deeply disturbed by the decline of the news media in America. The kind of reporting he did is now virtually extinct at local TV stations.

Decline of the News Media

To deal with declining profits and audiences, TV news at both the local and network levels have severely slashed both their staffs and their equipment. Webcams can save them so much money, they will soon be the norm for most local TV interviews.

So he wrote this book, to hopefully improve the quality of those encounters.

Job Interviews by Webcam

Webcams are also becoming standard as a screening tool for job interviews.

For job hunters, auditioning is stressful enough, without the added element of this new technology. Hopefully, this book will help level that playing field.

Starting as a Newspaper Reporter

Clarence started working for a daily newspaper when he was still in college. That career lasted 16 years (*Florida Times-Union* and *Jacksonville Journal* in Gainesville, Jacksonville, and Tallahassee. Then the *Miami Herald* in Miami and Washington, DC). He was the *Herald's* Washington correspondent when TV made him an offer he couldn't refuse.

TV Investigative Reporting

He was a television investigative reporter for 14 years (two years at WHAS-TV in Louisville, KY, 12 years at WPLG-TV in Miami). At WPLG, he won four Emmys and three duPont-Columbia Awards (TV's equivalent of the Pulitzer Prize). For many years, he was the only reporter for a local station who had ever won three duPont-Columbias.

Several other reporters have now matched that record.

Computer Pioneer

In December, 1968, he was the first reporter in the world to use a computer to crunch data for a series of stories analyzing Criminal Court cases for the *Miami Herald*.

Clarence has been a geek for most of his life. His specialty is explaining stuff so beginners can understand and become enthusiasts.

Photographer

He had a darkroom in the family bathroom when he was in the fifth grade. In his early days as a correspondent in a distant newspaper bureaus, he shot, developed and printed the photographs for his stories.

Then he transmitted them to the home office via an ancient telephone device that took 20 minutes per photo. True Stone-Age technology.

Building His Own Computers

He bought his first desktop computer in 1984. In 2006, he built a computer from scratch for the first time.

Winning with the News Media (his first book, now in its 9th Edition) is considered by many to be the "bible" in its field.

In addition to this book, his other current books (in both print and e-book formats) are:

Winning with the News Media - *A Self-Defense Manual When You're the Story*

They're Gonna Murder You - *War Stories From My Life at the News Front*

Sailboat Projects - *Clever Ideas and How to Make Them for a Pittance*

More Sailboat Projects (a sequel), and

Filming Family History - *How to Save Great Stories for Future Generations*

He frequently publishes magazine articles on sailing, photography, and home improvement ideas. Most are how-to pieces, showing creative, inexpensive ways to do or make something.

Contact Us

You can reach author Clarence Jones:

By e-mail:

cjones@winning-newsmedia.com

By snail mail:

Clarence Jones

6907 Vista Bella Drive

Bradenton, FL 34209

By Telephone:

941.779.0242

Help With Your Webcam

He's available to help with your webcam setup, and on-camera skills.

You can place a Skype call and talk to him on-camera. For a flat fee, he will critique your setup and make suggestions for improving it.

On-Camera Coaching

He's available to be your on-camera coach. He will role-play webcam interviews with you, helping you make your on-camera presence more effective.

He also works with clients to help them manage a crisis, or to prepare for a major presentation, news interview or news conference.

###

www.ingramcontent.com/pod-product-compliance
Lightning Source LLC
Chambersburg PA
CBHW051727170526
45167CB00002B/827